FE 2b/d
VS
ALBATROS SCOUTS

Western Front 1916–17

JAMES F. MILLER

First published in Great Britain in 2014 by Osprey Publishing
PO Box 883, Oxford, OX1 9PL, UK

PO Box 3985, New York, NY 10185-3985, USA

E-mail: info@ospreypublishing.com

A CIP catalogue record for this book is available from the British Library.

ISBN: 978 1 78096 325 9
PDF e-book ISBN: 978 1 78096 326 6
e-Pub ISBN: 978 1 78096 327 3

Edited by Tony Holmes
Cover artwork, cockpits, Engaging the Enemy and armament scrap views
by Jim Laurier
Battlescene by Mark Postlethwaite
Three-views by James F. Miller
Index by Marie-Pierre Evans
Typeset in Adobe Garamond Pro
Maps by Bounford.com
Originated by PDQ Digital Media Solutions, UK
Printed in China through Asia Pacific Offset Ltd

14 15 16 17 10 9 8 7 6 5 4 3 2 1

Osprey Publishing is supporting the Woodland Trust, the UK's leading
woodland conservation charity, by funding the dedication of trees.

www.ospreypublishing.com

FE 2b/d cover art

On 5 June *Jasta* 28 *Kommandeur* Ltn Karl-Emil Schaefer led a patrol of
Albatros scouts that intercepted several patrolling No. 20 Sqn FE 2ds.
Flying an Albatros DIII, the 30-victory ace attacked FE 2d A6384
NEWFOUNDLAND NO. 2, wounding its pilot, Lt W. W. Sawden,
who dived out of the fight. Briefly pursued by Schaefer, Sawden managed
an emergency landing near Ypres but died of his wounds. (*Artwork by
Jim Laurier*)

Albatros scout cover art

Meanwhile, fellow *Jasta* 28 pilot Max Müller observed that as Schaefer
pursued Sawden's fleeing FE 2d, his red Albatros was 'attacked by three more
[FE 2ds] from the rear and above'. Müller believed that Schaefer – whom he
opined was 'a man like Boelcke' – had been 'mistaken for von Richthofen',
and that 'for a long time the Englishmen had been planning to destroy the red
aircraft'. Likely protecting their comrade regardless of their pursuer's aeroplane
colour, an FE 2d flown by Lts Harold Satchell and Thomas Lewis entered a
protracted, descending curve fight with Schaefer until a 'long burst at very
close range' hit the D III, which according to Müller then 'broke up and
crashed vertically'. The famous ace was killed by the terrain impact,
becoming Satchell and Lewis's fourth victory. (*Artwork by Jim Laurier*)

Acknowledgements

The author wishes to thank the following for their selfless contributions –
Jim, Major and LaFonda Miller, Chris and Charyn Cordry, James G. and
Judy Miller, Tom and Karen Dillon, Lance Bronnenkant, Jon Guttman,
Jack Herris, Reinhard Kastner, Peter Kilduff, Herb and Sarah Kilmer,
the League of World War I Historians, Koloman Mayrhofer, David Peace,
Dr Mark Senft, Dr Gary Ordog, Marton Szigeti, Greg VanWyngarden,
Aaron Weaver and Reinhard Zankl.

Editor's Note

For ease of comparison between types, imperial measurements are used almost
exclusively throughout this book. The exception is weapon calibres, which are
given in their official designation, whether metric or imperial. The following
data will help in converting between imperial and metric measurements:

1 mile = 1.6km
1lb = 0.45kg
1yd = 0.9m
1ft = 0.3m
1in = 2.54cm/25.4mm
1 gallon (UK) = 4.55l
1 ton (UK) = 1.02 tonnes
1hp = 0.74kW

CONTENTS

INTRODUCTION

After World War I began in August 1914, the mobile conflict that everyone had expected lasted but a matter of weeks. Initially, the German forces caught the Entente off guard by violating established treaties and pushing through neutral Belgium, enabling them to swing behind the main French and British forces and head south in the direction of Paris. There were available units that attempted to thwart this invasion, but they were unable to stop the Germans until spirited counter-attacks were made during the Battle of the Marne from 5 to 10 September, which halted the advance some 30–40 miles shy of the French capital.

Already weakened by combat losses and far-stretched communications and supply lines, the Germans withdrew strategically and established defensive positions at the Aisne River. When these could not be breached the opposing forces attempted to outflank each other, building elaborate systems of defensive trenches as they moved further from Paris. These systems were eventually halted by the North Sea and Swiss border. Initially thought to be temporary, the trenches bordered a static front that saw very limited movement during the next four years.

With behind-the-lines reconnaissance incursions now throttled by the static positions of the entrenched armies, photo-reconnaissance via aeroplanes became increasingly important to provide strategists with real-time information and views of enemy forces that would not have been attainable otherwise. Although aeroplanes and aerial reconnaissance were still in their infancy, they had already proved their worth to the French by providing intelligence about troop movements that was used to formulate the counter-attack that stopped the initial German advance at the Marne. At first, these observation sorties flew unencumbered by enemy aerial interdiction, save for anti-aircraft fire, but soon the furtherance of reconnaissance sorties increased aerial encounters between the combatants.

Given that it was war, it was inevitable that crews would start taking weapons aloft with them in order to shoot at enemy aeroplanes they stumbled upon. Naturally, this led to aeroplanes being manufactured with defensive armament. Offensive armament developed as well, but it was hamstrung without effective means of utilising forward-firing weapons because of the spinning propeller. Thus, two expedients were employed – installing a forward-firing machine gun above the top wing that fired over the propeller, and the development of pusher aeroplanes (i.e., the engine and propeller were behind the crew, providing them with a wide, unencumbered forward field-of-fire). The French pursued both these avenues with their single-seat Nieuport scouts (which used over-wing machine guns) and two-seater Farmans (pusher configuration), while initially the British Royal Flying Corps (RFC) focused on two-seat pushers. The first of these was the Vickers FB 5 'Gunbus', its bathtub nacelle and braced-boom empennage duly inspiring the Germans to refer to any RFC pusher thereafter as a 'Vickers', regardless of true manufacturer.

The Germans, who eschewed over-wing weaponry and pusher designs, found themselves in the ascendancy by producing the first single-seat scouts armed with a machine gun that was synchronised to fire between the blades of a rotating propeller. This ability had an alarming impact on the RFC in 1915, both materially and psychologically, and ushered in a period of combat casualties that became known as the 'Fokker Scourge'. The Gunbus crews were gallant, but RFC commander Maj Gen Hugh Trenchard requested 'these machines be replaced by something better at an early date. Will you please say when you will be able to replace these machines with FE 2bs, powered by either 160hp Beardmore or Rolls-Royce engines, or some other type of machine'.

The aeroplane he requested, the Royal Aircraft Factory FE 2b, was developed in 1915, but its mass production had been stymied by delays with engine allocation.

No. 20 Sqn FE 2d A6516 shows off its triple-Lewis machine gun armament, comprised of two flexible weapons for the observer and the pilot's single fixed gun, which became standard on machines flown by the unit from June 1917. The bags dangling from these weapons collected spent cartridge cases and prevented them from impacting the sheathed, four-bladed propeller.

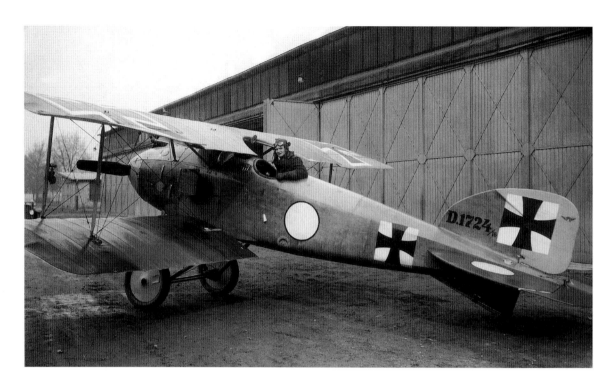

When FE 2bs began arriving in early 1916 they joined the British DH 2 and French Nieuport scouts, plunging headlong into battle against the synchronised German machines. By summer, they had bested the so-called 'Fokker Scourge'. However, by then Germany had already upped the ante by installing a Mercedes D III two-seater engine into a new single-seater design that resulted in enough power for unprecedented speed *and* capability to be armed with two synchronised machine guns, increasing both weight of fire and time of fire. Known as the Albatros D I, this new aeroplane entered the war in September 1916 and introduced a lineage that became Germany's main fighter for the next year and a half, although the service lives of the FE 2 and Albatros D-series overlapped for some 11 months only.

Despite the FE 2's performance being outclassed by the Albatros, the aeroplane's crews had no choice but to engage the superior fighter because RFC offensive strategy sent them into German territory day after day. Yet they did so unwaveringly, learning well and developing tactics to overcome the performance discrepancy. Always, they fought tenaciously. Many went down before the guns of Albatros scouts – Manfred von Richthofen, Germany's 'Red Baron', is credited with 13 FE 2s – but many Albatrosses were also downed by their ungainly foes. One celebrated FE 2d crew was credited with shooting down 15 Albatros D IIIs in a five-week period, and some of Germany's top aces were killed or wounded fighting the aggressive 'Fees', including Max Immelmann (killed prior to Albatros availability, flying a Fokker E III), Karl Schaefer and Manfred von Richthofen.

In the end, although the ageing heavyweight had stood toe-to-toe with the up-and-coming contender, ultimately it was technology that triumphed, forcing the RFC to throw in the towel. Not so much as a matter of defeat, but as a consequence of that war's hyper-rapid technological advancements. By today's standards, the quest for

victory compressed decades of advancement into solitary years. Designed in 1915, the FE 2 had simply flown beyond its useful life just two years later.

Similarly, the Albatros existed in a state of flux, with six new models released within its first year of service life in a chase to achieve performance increases it never attained. Although it served until war's end, the Albatros had been superseded in the frontline by the next generation of German fighter – the Fokker D VII – come the spring of 1918.

No. 100 Sqn FE 2b A5478 *GOLD COAST No 10* was painted black overall and employed as a night bomber after its daylight usefulness had expired. Such FE 2bs employed V-strut undercarriages to permit the installation of a 230lb bomb and rack.

CHRONOLOGY

1911

August — Geoffrey de Havilland conducts first FE 2 trials.

1914

June — Albatros Type DD wins 100km speed prize at the *Aspern Flugmeeting* in Vienna. Designed by Ernst Heinkel and Robert Thelen, the Type DD is considered to be the forerunner of the Albatros Ds.

28 June — Archduke Franz Ferdinand of Austria assassinated by Serbian student Gavrilo Princip, beginning a period of international diplomatic manoeuvring.

July — To end Serbian interference in Bosnia, Austria-Hungary delivers a ten-demand ultimatum to Serbia, intentionally made to be unacceptable and provoke war. Serbia agrees to eight demands.

28 July — Austria-Hungary declares war on Serbia.

29 July — Russian Empire orders partial mobilisation in support of Serbia.

30 July — German Empire delivers ultimatum to Russia to cease mobilisation against Austria-Hungary.

1 August — France orders mobilisation and Germany declares war on Russia.

3 August — Germany declares war on France and invades Belgium.

4 August — UK declares war on Germany in support of Belgian neutrality. World War I fully underway.

1915

26 January — FE 2a makes first flight.

Summer — German monoplanes armed with synchronised machine guns plunder RFC reconnaissance two-seaters, begetting the 'Fokker Scourge'.

2 October — First FE 2b completed.

1916

January — FE 2bs arrive in France *en masse* with No. 20 Sqn.

7 April — First FE 2d flight. Machine is 10mph faster and has an 8,000ft higher ceiling than FE 2b.

FE 2b 6937 *PUNJAB 29 RAWALPINDI* of No. 18 Sqn was forced down by German fighters on 22 September 1916. This machine featured two Lewis machine guns, a modified undercarriage, 120hp Beardmore engine and a two-bladed propeller.

June	Thelen design team's Albatros D I undergoes flight evaluation and static load tests at Adlershof.
18 June	German 15-victory ace Max Immelmann is killed in action flying a Fokker E III against FE 2bs, an event that is generally regarded as marking the end of the 'Fokker Scourge'.
July	Albatros D I ordered into production.
1 July	The Battle of the Somme commences. British forces suffer 60,000 killed or wounded on the first day of the offensive.
August	Germans implement the *Jagdstaffel*, a dedicated group of single-seat fighters tasked primarily with hunting enemy two-seater reconnaissance and artillery-spotting machines.
16 September	Albatros D Is and a single D II arrive in-field with *Jagdstaffel* 2. Ltn Otto Höhne shoots down the first FE 2b.
Late December	Albatros D IIIs begin arriving at front-line *Jagdstaffeln*.

1917

27 January	Structural failures of new Albatros D III lower wings forces *Idflieg* to ground the new aeroplanes until they are either reinforced or repaired.
19 February	*Idflieg* rescinds Albatros D III ground order.
March	No. 100 Sqn becomes first FE 2b night-bombing squadron to reach France. FE 2bs in this and other units serve in this capacity until the Armistice.
April	Battle of Arras introduces period of intense RFC casualties known as 'Bloody April'.
May	Albatros D V begin arriving at frontline *Jagdstaffeln*.
5 June	*Jasta* 28 *Staffelführer* Karl Schaefer shot down and killed fighting No. 20 Sqn FE 2ds.
6 July	Manfred von Richthofen suffers ricochet gunshot wound to the head during large aerial battle with No. 20 Sqn FE 2ds. Although far from mortal, this wound effectively removes him from combat for the majority of the remaining year.
August	No. 20 Sqn is the last frontline unit equipped with FE 2s for daylight use.
17 August	No. 20 Sqn records last FE 2 victory.

Its spinning propeller gleaming, a chocked *Jasta* 2 Albatros D I at Lagnicourt warms up before an afternoon sortie in the autumn of 1916. As was *Jasta* 2 practice, the fuselage has been darkly overpainted up to the front annular engine cowl, with a 'wash' over the national insignia.

DESIGN AND DEVELOPMENT

RAF FE 2

The second FE 2 featured a 70hp air-cooled V8 Renault engine and the wing design from a BE 2a, but had no fin and was never armed. This machine was destroyed in a crash in February 1914.

The development of the Royal Aircraft Factory (hereafter referred to as RAF, not to be confused with the Royal Air Force, which came into existence on 1 April 1918, beyond the frame of this work) FE 2b began with a £1,000 investment procured by future RAF aeroplane designer Geoffrey de Havilland. Born on 27 July 1882, de Havilland had graduated from the Crystal Palace Engineering School in 1903 and worked as a motor engineering draughtsman in Birmingham and then at a London bus construction company.

Intrigued by reports of heavier-than-air aviation feats and accomplishments on the continent, de Havilland and partner Frank Hearle quit their jobs so that they could build their own aeroplane. Financed by the £1,000 investment from de Havilland's grandfather, the partners accomplished their goal in 1909 – the machine was destroyed on its first

take-off, with de Havilland at the controls. He was uninjured.

The next year the partners assembled a second machine that was flown successfully – its first flight was also de Havilland's first. A Farman-type pusher biplane (an 'F Class', so designated by His Majesty's Balloon Factory Superintendent Mervyn Joseph Pius O'Gorman as 'Those [aeroplanes] which have the main wings followed

The third FE 2a, 2864. Its original powerplant was a 100hp water-cooled Green engine, but this was replaced by 120hp Austro-Daimler, modified by Beardmore. This engine proved so successful that the Beardmore was given the 'green light' for use in further aeroplane production.

by a smaller plane more lightly loaded, but the propellers of which are placed between the main wings and the tailplane') with a forward elevator, de Havilland used the machine to teach himself how to fly. He was then offered a position as designer and test pilot with His Majesty's Balloon Factory, forerunner of the Royal Aircraft Factory. De Havilland then sold his pusher to the War Office, although the sale was subject to demonstration that it could fly for one hour without need for maintenance. This was conducted successfully in January 1911, although de Havilland had to land twice during that time in order to 'thaw out' due to the frigid winter weather.

After this sale de Havilland's aeroplane was designated the FE 1 (Farman Experimental 1), and it underwent continual refinement throughout the spring. This included new streamlined struts, increased tailplane area, wing extensions, larger rudder, the removal of the front elevator and re-rigging to adjust the centre of gravity.

De Havilland conducted many successful passenger flights with the FE 1, but on 15 August the factory's Assistant Superintendent Lt Theodore Ridge – who had begun learning to fly just weeks before – crashed the machine while landing. He was uninjured but the FE 1 never flew again.

Fortuitously, the very next day de Havilland made his first flight in his new design, the FE 2, which was of a similar pusher configuration as the FE 1 but employed a fabric-covered nacelle and 50hp Gnome rotary engine. After about a month of tweaking and overcoming teething troubles with the engine, de Havilland flew the machine cross-country in furtherance of securing his Superior Aviator's Certificate, and by year's end he was taking the FE 2 up to nearly 2000ft. In the first half of 1912 the FE 2 was fitted with floats for experiments as a 'Hydro-Aeroplane'. Several successful flights were conducted, after which the 50hp Gnome was replaced by one of 70hp, allowing a passenger to be carried.

The focus then shifted to arming the FE 2 with a machine gun. The aeroplane was well suited for such weaponry in the era prior to reliable gun synchronisation as its rear-mounted engine and propeller eliminated the problem of trying to fire a weapon through a spinning propeller arc without shooting the blades off. A belt-fed Maxim machine gun was installed to the forward nacelle, but tests revealed a limited range of elevation that would require a variable-height pivot point mount for the gun to be used effectively. In 1913 a second FE 2 was built that featured a larger streamlined nacelle, a 70hp Renault V8 engine and the same wings as employed by the tractor-powered BE 2. However, in February 1914 this machine spun in and crashed, injuring the RAF's Chief Test Pilot Ronald Kemp (who had replaced de Havilland in that capacity

FE 2d

31ft 9in

47ft 9in

after the latter's departure in March for the Aircraft Manufacturing Company) and killing his passenger.

Armed with knowledge amassed from the previous FE designs, the RAF, in mid-1914, designed and built the FE 2a. Created with the intention of being a 'Gun-Carrier', it was larger and heavier than its forerunners and featured a three-bay wing design attached to a large nacelle that housed the two-man crew and a 100hp water-cooled Green engine. The trailing edge of the centre section wings was hinged as an air brake. The landing gear consisted of oleo struts, which were comprised of oil and air pistons designed to expand and contract and absorb shock from landing and operating out of rough fields. A smaller 'buffer' nose wheel was attached to prevent nose-over only – the aeroplane was not of 'tricycle' gear configuration. A tailskid supported the empennage, making the FE 2a a proper 'tail dragger.'

Twelve FE 2as were ordered, arriving in January 1915, but the Green engine was too heavy for its power output and was replaced by a 120hp Beardmore, which had originally been an Austro-Daimler design – Beardmore boosted its power output through the fitment of dual magnetos and carburettors. The first two FE 2as were fitted with the Green engine, but from the third production machine onwards the aeroplane employed the new engine. Production delays in the Beardmore factory ran downhill, however, slowing up the delivery of FE 2as to the RFC. Indeed, the 12th, and last, example was finally delivered in early October, this aeroplane boasting wings of a new airfoil section, a conventional V-strut undercarriage and no airbrake. The 12 FE 2as saw service in France, with pilots reporting that they were easy to fly, easy to land, stable in flight and fitted with a comfortable cockpit.

Impressed with the FE 2a, the War Office requested that the aeroplane be produced by a handful of contractors, including Boulton & Paul, Richard Garrett & Sons, Ransome, Sims & Jeffries and G. & J. Weir, Ltd. Various design refinements and upgrades seen on the last FE 2a led to the new machine being designated the FE 2b. The FE 2a wing centre section was retained but the inboard trailing edges of the lower stub wings were rounded at the nacelle junction and the centre-section airbrake was permanently removed. The radiator was mounted between the pilot and the engine and was fed by cooling air ducted via adjustable doors that faired smoothly against the fuselage when closed. A steerable tailskid was also fitted. As with the FE 2a, the new aeroplane was fitted with a V-shaped tricycle undercarriage in place of draggy oleo struts. However, an in-field compromise known as the Trafford Jones undercarriage (named after its creator) provided the shock absorption oleo struts but retained the improved aerodynamics of the V-strut.

With the FE 2b's aerodynamics hampered by the inherently draggy booms, struts and associated rigging, calls arose to increase the aeroplane's speed through the fitting of a more powerful engine. A 160hp Beardmore was under development but was hamstrung by reliability and construction failures. In January 1916 the RAF proposed the FE 2 be fitted with a 250hp Rolls-Royce V12. As the nomenclature designated, this engine – which came to be known as the Eagle – employed two parallel rows of six steel cylinders affixed in a 'V' configuration to an aluminium crankcase, with an epicyclical reduction gear that reduced propeller rpm to about two-thirds that of the crankshaft, increasing propeller efficiency. The airframe was unchanged, save for modifications to mount the new engine and a redesigned fuel tank that replaced the 24-gallon cylindrical

Unarmed FE 2b A5666 illustrates the classic shape of this variant, with the high-back pilot cockpit, outer wing dihedral, internal radiator vertical air scoops (adjacent the pilot cockpit) and Trafford Jones undercarriage modification.

fuel tank with a 36-gallon rectangular one. The new variant became the FE 2d, which boasted a better rate-of-climb, higher ceiling and faster top speed.

Earlier, the RAF had experimented with a more streamlined nacelle in which the cockpits for the pilot and observer were reversed, giving the pilot access to a forward-firing Lewis gun and increased visibility. The latter was considered especially useful during landing, thus the buffer nose wheel was removed and a 'V' type undercarriage installed. This variant became known as the FE 2c. The repositioned observer retained a wide field of fire, but owing to his closer proximity to the wings he could no longer fire rearward up and above them. One FE 2c was eventually fitted with an oleo undercarriage and used by the RAF for testing bombsights until it crashed in May 1917, while another served in France with Nos. 22 and 25 Sqns until it was destroyed in a landing accident that July. This variant never entered production.

Although FE 2s duelled with the Albatros during daylight operations, the type was also pressed into service as a night bomber. This required a fuel tank alteration to carry an additional ten gallons, and some FE 2bs were fitted with a second gravity tank under the centre section of the upper wing. The 230lb bomb rack prohibited use of the Trafford Jones undercarriage and thus V-struts were employed. A chute was installed for parachute flares, navigation lights were affixed to the lower wingtips and Holt's flares were mounted below the wings that provided ground illumination when landing at night.

No. 20 Sqn FE 2d A19 illustrates some visual differences from the similar-looking FE 2b, including cut-down pilot cockpit fairing and external radiator. Note the asbestos-wrapped centre section struts and originally configured undercarriage.

During several different production runs, 1,929 FE 2as and FE 2bs were built by the previously mentioned contractors. Two FE 2cs were built by the RAF. The total number of FE 2ds built is unknown. Some 248 were delivered to the RFC, of which 183 went to France, 25 to Home Defence, and 40 to training units. The RAF also developed FE 2e, f, g and h models of varying configurations, but none entered production (indeed the FE 2f and g are believed to have never progressed beyond the design stage) and they are not relevant to this work.

ALBATROS D I TO D V

For much of the first decade of the 20th century Germany's aviation aspirations focused on lighter rather than heavier-than-air flight, although new heavier-than-air machines were not unknown. In 1905 the Americans Orville and Wilbur Wright brought their aeroplane to Europe to demonstrate controlled powered flight, and showed its practicality via a flight of 39km.

While the *Kriegsministerium* (War Ministry) conference of 1906 established that military aeronautics ought to focus on rigid airships, in large part due to their familiarity with lighter-than-air machines versus the newer heavier-than-air machines, 1909 saw a boon in the interest and development of the aeroplane. Public money was used to promote aeroplane development, demonstration flights were conducted and the first German flight meeting took place at the country's inaugural aerodrome at Johannisthal, near Berlin.

Although various manufacturers came to Johannisthal and, under licence, began building aeroplanes of foreign design, in October 1909 a 3km flight made at the aerodrome netted the pilot a 40,000 Deutschmark prize for the first flight of a German aeroplane powered by a German aero engine. Lighter-than-air machines still retained the focus of the German military, but many people realised that the aeroplane was coming of age. One such individual was German biologist Dr Walther Huth, who had established his own company (*Albatros Flugzeugwerke GmbH*, named after the seabird with which he was familiar from his previous scientific studies) at Johannisthal that December.

The unarmed Albatros D I prototype at Johannisthal. Note the clear-doped-linen rudder, horizontal stabilisers, elevator and lower wings. This machine closely resembles the production configuration D I. Indeed, the only things unique to the prototype were the upturned exhaust manifold, unbalanced elevator, externally routed rudder cables and no windscreen. (Reinhard Zankl)

With foresight enough to recognise the aeroplane's future importance to the military, Huth contacted the *Kriegsministerium* in October 1909 and offered the services of his aeroplanes forthe purpose of flight instruction. Negotiations with the *Militärbehörde* (military authority) lasted until March 1910, when they accepted Huth's proposal. It is believed flight instruction began that July, and training continued as Albatros was contracted to build lattice-framed Farman reproductions with the type designation Albatros MZ 2.

ALBATROS DV

24ft 2in

9ft 0in

29ft 6in

In 1912 Albatros hired *Diplom-Ingenieur* (Engineering Graduate) Robert Thelen as chief designer. Teaming up with *Dipl. Ing.* Helmut Hirth (FAI-Brevet 79 from 11 March 1911) and employing the perfected semi-monocoque wooden fuselage designs of *Ober-Ingenieur* Hugo Grohmann (a construction technique which provided enough strength via the external skin to eliminate the need for internal bracing, thereby reducing weight and increasing performance and payload capacity), Thelen's designs moved away from the Farman-type open-lattice construction as Albatros began building newly designed aeroplanes with the type of enclosed wooden fuselages (*Rumpf-Doppeldecker*, or fuselage double-decker [biplane]) for which they would become renowned.

After World War I broke fully in August 1914, Albatros concentrated on manufacturing two-seat B- and C-type machines. Aerial observation and artillery spotting were crucial for the support of ground forces, and this in turn meant that these types received manufacturing and engine allocation priority.

Naturally, as the war progressed, the opposing forces developed single-seat fighters to protect their two-seater observation machines and destroy those of the enemy. These fighters had, in the main, been powered by rotary engines. Those powered by inline engines had been somewhat hamstrung by a lack of available higher horsepower engines, which were prioritised for the B- and C-type machines. This did not lessen the born-from-experience calls from fighter pilots requesting that single-engined machines be equipped with higher horsepower motors and armed with two rather than the then-standard single machine gun.

Rather than compete with the manoeuvrability of the more nimble French Nieuports and British DH 2s, which not only out-flew the German Fokker and Pfalz E-type wing-warping monoplanes but were present in greater numbers, the Thelen-led Albatros design bureau set to work on what became the Albatros D I. By April 1916 it had developed a sleek yet rugged machine that featured the usual Albatros semi-monocoque wooden construction and employed a 160hp Mercedes D III engine with power enough to equip the aeroplane with two forward-firing machine guns. Visual hallmarks of the D I and early production D II include fuselage mounted Windhoff radiators and matching chords for the upper and lower wings.

Port-forward view of the unarmed pre-production Albatros D II. It is already equipped with a centrally-located wing radiator, although early D II production featured side-mounted Windhoff radiators. When equipped with machine guns, a new windscreen and serial number 386/16, this machine became the personal mount of *Jagdstaffel* 2 *Staffelführer* Hptm Oswald Boelcke from 16 September 1916. He died in this aeroplane six weeks later.

Concurrent with the development of the D I, Thelen's team had also designed and constructed a second machine that was similar to the D I, the Albatros D II. It is important to note that these machines evolved simultaneously, and that the D II was not the result of post-combat pilot feedback from D I pilots. Proof is found not only in photographs but also in the pre-production order of 12 machines, of which one was D II 386/16 (which became legendary German ace Oswald Boelcke's machine, as will be seen) and one (D.388/16) was a prototype Albatros D III.

Essentially, the D I and D II were the same machine with several noticeable external differences and improvements. The D I's inverted V-strut centre-section pylon had been replaced by outwardly splayed N-struts, improving forward visibility, the wing gap was reduced by lowering the upper wing 9.8 inches (250mm), which also improved forward and upper visibility and the side-mounted Windhoff radiators were replaced with a Teeves & Braun wing-mounted radiator located between the new struts. This final modification did not take effect until after the first production run of 50 D IIs (excluding Boelcke's pre-production D II 386/16, which was built with a wing-mounted radiator), which made up the second half of *Idflieg's* first order for 100 Albatros fighters (50 D Is, 422–471/16, and 50 D IIs, 472–521/16).

In August 50 more D IIs (890–939/16) were ordered from Huth's *Ostdeutsche Albatros Werke* (OAW, an independent firm at the time that would be assimilated into the main Albatros company October 1917), located in Schneidmühl. These machines were designated Albatros D II (OAW) and constructed nearly identically to those built at Johannisthal, as were the 75 machines (1024–1098/16) to be built under licence by LVG *Luftverkehrsgesellschaft* (LVG), also ordered in August. September saw Albatros receive the final D II production order for 100 machines (1700–1799/16), after which production focus shifted to the next generation of Albatros fighters, the D III (see *Osprey Duel 36 – SPAD VII vs Albatros D III* for further details).

Designed to increase the Albatros scout's manoeuvrability and improve the pilot's downward vision, the D III was heavily influenced by flight tests carried out on captured French Nieuports. Like these nimble French aeroplanes, the D III employed a sesquiplane design (technically, a biplane having one wing with not more than half the area of the other wing, this designation is often used to denote an aeroplane with a lower wing that is much smaller than the upper, even though more than half the area) that featured a single rather than dual-spar lower wing of reduced chord. This required the fore and aft interplane struts to be connected with one another at the lower wings' single spar, creating the classic 'V-strut' configuration of all subsequent production Albatros D-types.

However, the sesquiplane design led to structural failures of the D III's lower wings within the first weeks of its arrival at frontline units in January 1917. After several close calls and even deaths as the result of these failures, on 27 January 1917 *Idflieg* (*Inspektion der Fliegertruppen*, or Inspectorate of Aviation Troops) grounded all Albatros D IIIs until their wings were replaced by stronger ones or their current wings reinforced in-field by sheet metal braces that Albatros had already been supplying by the time of *Idflieg's* grounding. The grounding lasted until 19 February, and production orders continued for further D IIIs, but wing failures continued to plague the machines and pilots were aware that prolonged power dives invited

Early Albatros D V production machines, of which 1021/17 was the 22nd, featured an oft-disliked headrest that many pilots removed – its manufacture was quickly discontinued. Regarded as a lighter but less robust D III, the D V enjoyed equal performance but disappointed pilots who expected more.

catastrophe. Regardless of these problems, the Albatros D III was enormously successful. By the end of April 1917, it accounted for nearly 50 per cent of all frontline D-types, with the Albatros D II comprising another 25 per cent.

Even with such success and numbers, Albatros's efforts to improve the fighter never halted, and thus by April 1917 two new D-types had been ordered into concurrent production that ran until late 1917. The first was a continuation of the D III, built by OAW and designated the Albatros D III (OAW). This machine appeared nearly identical to the Johannisthal-built D III – the most noticeable visual difference was a curved rather than vertical trailing edge to the rudder – but with airframe construction and strengthening refinements.

With OAW continuing the D III output, Albatros's Johannisthal facilities concentrated on production of the D V (the D IV was a test bed designed to evaluate a geared version of the Mercedes engine, which was completely housed within the fuselage and gave the D IV a very streamlined appearance – this design also reverted to the twin-spar biplane configuration of the D II). The D V was another redesign of the series, although this time changes centred on the fuselage, rather than the engine and wings. With the D V, Albatros abandoned the slab-sided fuselage for one that was ovoid throughout its length, reducing the machine's form drag and easing construction. As with the D III (OAW), it employed a curved rudder. Early D Vs of the first production batch also featured a large headrest that proved to be unpopular – it was often removed in the field, and was eventually eliminated from production.

Unfortunately, the D V experienced further wing structural problems, and although the fifth D-type incarnation in less than a year, pilots were disappointed because it offered essentially the same performance as the previous Albatros scouts. Of these latter types, *Idflieg* reported, 'The Albatros D III [OAW] is more robustly constructed than the D V. The D V is merely regarded as a lightened D III. The performance of both is equal. The D V will not be manufactured further, only the D III'.

In August and September 1917, production orders were initiated for the penultimate and final versions of production Albatros D-types, the D V and D Va (OAW). No fewer than 1,062 D Vas and 600 OAWs were built, but by the time of their frontline arrival the FE 2b/d had been removed from service as a fighter – although it was employed in training and night-bombing capacities – and they saw few, if any, encounters with these last two Albatros D-types.

TECHNICAL SPECIFICATIONS

RAF FE 2b/d

The RAF FE 2 arose from the need for aeroplanes armed with forward-firing machine guns when the unreliability of synchronisation gear that permitted gunfire through a spinning propeller arc necessitated such machines be pusher designs – i.e., engine at the rear. The standard engine used by the FE 2b was the 120hp Beardmore, a normally aspirated, water-cooled, six-cylinder inline engine. The fuel and oil tanks (24 and four gallons, respectively) were housed within the nacelle, with an eight-gallon gravity tank mounted directly to the undersurface of the centre upper wing, offset to starboard. Endurance was 2.5 hours.

A desire for increased performance and endurance led to the installation of a 160hp Beardmore, but these suffered from overheating and the failure of bolts that held the cylinders to the crankcase. Rather than wait for Beardmore to sort these teething troubles, the RAF Factory proposed the FE 2d, which employed a 12-cylinder Rolls-Royce V12 Eagle engine, rated at 250hp.

The aeroplane was largely unchanged, but its 'bathtub' nacelle had to be modified to accept the new engine and an associated larger fuel tank of 36 gallons, the shape of which was squared from the original cylindrical tank and fitted beneath the pilot's seat. The radiator was moved from an internal nacelle location between the cockpit and

FE 2d REAR COCKPIT

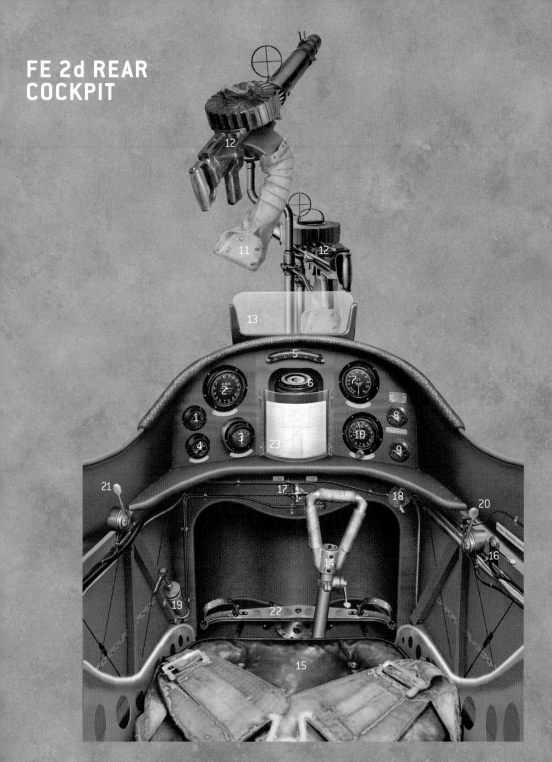

1. Clock
2. Tachometer
3. Air pressure gauge
4. Radiator temperature gauge
5. Inclinometer
6. Magnetic compass
7. Airspeed indicator
8. Starting magneto

9. Magneto switch
10. Altimeter
11. Ejected link bag
12. Lewis 0.303in. machine gun
13. Windscreen
14. Control column and spade grip
15. Pilot's seat
16. Radiator control lever

17. Transfer air selector valve
18. Transfer air selector switch
19. Priming pump
20. Mixture control lever
21. Throttle lever
22. Rudder bar
23. Map holder

No. 25 Sqn FE 2b 6341 *THE SCOTCH EXPRESS (ZANZIBAR NO. 1* on the port side) did not duel with any Albatros scouts, having been forced down four months prior to their arrival in the frontline, yet this post-capture photograph provides an excellent view of FE 2b armament.

engine to an external position behind the pilot, where it received direct contact of the cooling slipstream rather than requiring air to be ducted to it internally as with the FE. 2b. Unfortunately, the new radiator was too large and it cooled the engine excessively. Manually activated shutters that blocked airflow helped, but increased pilot workload. Ultimately, radiators identical to the type used by the Beardmore engine were fitted in their place. The shutters remained to facilitate engine warm-up, however.

The fixed pitch, two-blade propeller fitted to the 120hp FE 2b was constructed of glued mahogany laminations that sometimes included walnut. In April 1916 tests showed the efficiency of a four-bladed propeller, and thereafter 160hp FE 2bs and all FE 2ds were so equipped. Since a pusher's three-point configuration brought its rotating propeller blades in close proximity to the ground, where they were more susceptible to damage from stones and pebbles than propeller blades of tractor-powered aeroplanes, the leading edges and tips of the propeller blades were reinforced with doped fabric or brass sheaths.

The FE 2b's firepower generally consisted of two flexible Lewis 0.303in. machine guns installed in the observer's front cockpit, with rates of fire of approximately 550 rounds per minute. Gun mounts were numerous and varied, but commonly employed a forward mount that afforded a wide range of fire, while a second telescopic mount was situated between the tandem cockpits that could be elevated vertically to fire a Lewis rearwards over the top of the upper wing. The booms, propeller, wings, empennage and late-model upper wing gravity tank greatly hampered the rearward gun's cone of fire, and this mount only enabled effective defence against high-side rear attacks.

Manning either gun position required the observer to be unbelted and assume various hazardous stances as required by enemy proximity – cumbersome positions made more so by the relative wind, heavy flight clothes, combat manoeuvring and mental awareness of one's precarious proximity to an accidental multi-thousand-foot free-fall to certain death.

In his classic book *Horses Don't Fly*, Capt Frederick Libby ably described his first impression of these gun positions upon arriving at No. 23 Sqn:

The ship that was rolled out was the pusher type [an FE 2b], with the propeller in the rear. The pilot was in front of the motor in the middle of the ship and the observer in front of the pilot. When you stood, all of you from the knees up was exposed to the world. There was no [seat]belt and nothing to hold on to except the gun and sides of the nacelle. Fastened to the bottom and toward the front of the nacelle was a hollow steel rod with a specially fitted swivel mount for anchoring the machine gun, which could be swung from side to side or to the front as the occasion demanded, giving it a wonderful field-of-fire.

Between the observer and pilot was another gun, which was for the purpose of fighting a rear-run action over the top wing to protect your tail. The mounting consisted of a hollow steel rod, into which a solid steel rod was fitted to work up and down with the machine gun on the top. To operate this you simply pull the gun up as high as possible, where it locks into the fitting, then you step out of the nacelle and stand with a foot on each side. From this position you have nothing to worry about, except being blown out of the ship or being tossed out if the pilot makes a wrong move. This gun, I know, I am not going to like much. Brother, no wonder they need observers!

Such intimidations were soon overcome, as revealed by No. 20 Sqn observer Lt William Cambray:

On one occasion I was with a new – but good – pilot who had not previously been in a fight. A Hun dived down from our rear and I could see his tracer bullets going under us as I stood up to [fire] over the tail. I signalled to the pilot to throw the machine about to get rid of him, but to my surprise he only did a simple aerodrome-style turn. On returning to the aerodrome I asked my pilot in no uncertain terms why he had not thrown the machine all over the place. 'I was afraid I'd chuck you out', he answered. I replied that it was my job to stay in.

No. 20 Sqn's FE 2ds also employed a third Lewis that was fixed to fire forward by the pilot, the weight of which could be born by the Rolls-Royce engine. Its fitment was little doubt precipitated by pilots demanding more convenient firepower at their fingertips. An example of this was exhibited by future RFC luminary Maj Lanoe Hawker, whose observer in No. 6 Sqn noted that when flying FE 2bs, Hawker 'had a foul habit of carrying an ordinary rifle which he used to loose off if he didn't think I was doing too well. The noise just over my head was most alarming and annoying'. The Lewis machine guns were fed ammunition via a top-mounted rotating drum that contained 47 rounds (later 'double drums' held 97), and normally ten drums were carried aloft. A canvas deflector bag

An FE 2d during the winter of 1916–17. In addition to the Lewis gun, the aeroplane's external radiator and shutters are clearly visible (as is the sign *NO WATER IN RADIATOR*). Note also the underwing bomb racks, under-nacelle generator and starboard side camera battens adjacent to the observer's cockpit.

FE 2 FUSELAGE GUNS

The RAF FE 2 was armed with two air-cooled Lewis machine guns that were positioned on various flexible mounts and poles and fired by the observer. A gas-operated automatic weapon, the Lewis fired 0.303in. ammunition at a rate of approximately 550 rounds per minute. Bullets were stored in circular 47 or 97 cartridge magazines (or 'drums') that required changing by the observer in combat. Additionally, some FE 2ds were outfitted with a third Lewis positioned to starboard that was fixed for forward firing by the pilot.

attached to the Lewis caught spent cartridge cases lest they foul the cockpit or blow back into the propeller to damage it.

The FE 2b was produced with a No. 1 Mk II gun mount, but its small field-of-fire inspired various replacements. The standard front mount became the No. 4 Mk I, which was a fixed pillar attached to the nacelle frame. This was replaced by a No. 4 Mk III mount, which permitted lateral movement about a horizontal tube, until superseded by the No. 4 Mk IV mount. The latter had the pillar mounted to a universal joint on the cockpit floor. For rearward defence the FE 2 employed an 'Anderson Arch', which was a telescopic L-bent pillar that could be raised to fire a Lewis over the upper wing and the propeller arc.

All of the above was housed within a 'bathtub' nacelle framed with metal tubes and wooden formers that were in turn covered with aluminium panels, louvred on FE 2ds to promote engine crankcase cooling, and sides of laced fabric. Originally, the floor was to be armoured, but plywood was standard. The pilot sat in the upper rear cockpit, which was quite roomy, with the observer occupying the bulbous and slightly lower forward cockpit that provided a large field-of-fire. Pilot instrumentation included an altimeter, airspeed indicator, tachometer, bubble inclinometer, air pressure valve and gauge, oil pulsator glasses and compass. A conventional rudder bar and control column with a 'spade' grip provided pilot control about the axes.

Due to the FE 2's pusher configuration its crews received no warming benefits from residual engine heat, although the FE 2b's internal radiator warmed the pilot's back. The FE 2d nacelle was extended to accommodate the Rolls-Royce Eagle engine and repositioned radiator, and this led to the pilot's cockpit being moved forward and separated from the observer's cockpit by a single panel, onto which was mounted the pilot's flight instruments and fuel valves. This panel also employed a glazed centre section to aid pilot visibility.

A photomontage of the various FE 2 undercarriage configurations. They are, from top to bottom, the tricycle oleo, Trafford Jones modification and the V-strut, which required the elevator horns to be bent outwards to clear the forward struts.

Aerodynamic lift was provided by four subtly tip-tapered wings of equal span and chord, which used the same airfoils as the BE 2c. The wings were rigged without stagger or sweepback, but employed 3.5 degrees of dihedral. All were identical, and thus could be fitted in any port/starboard/upper/lower positions. The lower wings attached to centre section wing 'stubs' affixed to the nacelle, while the upper wings attached to a centre cabane section that connected to the nacelle via spruce struts just aft of the cockpit. The wings featured dual spar construction with an internally braced spruce frame and three-ply ribs enveloped within a skin of doped fabric. An aileron of similar construction was affixed to the outboard trailing edges of all four wings, which enabled pilot control about the longitudinal axis.

In lieu of a fuselage the FE 2 had a common-for-pushers arrangement of twin upper and lower wire-braced and strut-supported tubular wooden booms that bracketed the propeller and extended back to the empennage, where the upper and

lower booms attached in a V at the vertical rudder post. The empennage consisted of a horizontal stabiliser located atop the upper booms. A small, triangular vertical stabiliser was created above that by covering the rudder kingpost with fabric. The elevators and balanced rudder were similarly constructed and controlled by the pilot via cables that led to the cockpit, and the entire horizontal stabiliser angle of incidence could be ground-adjusted. The empennage was supported by a spring-cushioned, steerable steel-shoed tailskid copied from the BE 2.

The FE 2b's main undercarriage featured Oleo struts connected to a diminutive 'buffer' nose wheel designed for rollover protection. The oleo struts were highly effective at absorbing shock and the roughness of operating out of French fields, and this attribute was greatly appreciated by pilots. One such individual was Capt Cecil Lewis, who recalled decades later in his book *Farewell to Wings*:

> The most striking thing about this aeroplane [the FE 2b] was its famous 'oleo' undercart. I suppose this was the first time that telescopic oil buffers had ever been used to absorb landing shocks. The thing worked all right, but in the air the two legs hung down, fully extended, in a very limp and gawky manner – they looked as if they were tied on to the rest of the structure with string and might, at any moment, fall off.
>
> On landing, while the FE 2b was still six feet up, the wheels touched the ground with a long chattering rumble, and as the weight of the aircraft came down on them they gradually telescoped and took up the strain. It was almost impossible to make a bad landing with an FE 2b, so beautifully did those giraffe-like legs cushion and touch down.

Although effective for shock absorption, the oleo struts created much drag – they were soon replaced by a simple and conventional 'V'-strut configuration. These struts were not as well liked, however, leading No. 20 Sqn pilot Lt Trafford Jones to modify the oleo undercarriage by removing the nose wheel, and its associated struts, and angling the main gear's horizontal radius rods that used to be attach to the nose wheel upwards to attach to the now absent nose wheel strut connection points. Naturally named the 'Trafford Jones Modification', this configuration gave nearly the same reduced drag of the V-struts while retaining the shock absorption of the oleo struts. In June 1916 the RFC made a request to the RAF that all future FE 2bs should employ this modification.

FE 2s were fitted to carry various bombs throughout their careers. Even when on offensive patrol as fighting 'battleplanes' they often carried bombs to a pre-designated target before searching for enemy aeroplanes within their assigned patrol areas. FE 2 battleplanes had rails under the lower wings to which racks could be affixed that carried an assortment of bombs or flares, with four 20lb Cooper bombs common per side. Night bombers with V-strut landing gear could carry a single 230lb bomb on a cradle between the wheels. In-field experience led to frequent modifications of bomb racks and produced a host of different ordnance configurations. Whatever the payload, bombs were aimed via the CFS Mk 4b bombsight, mounted either to port or starboard, depending upon whether the pilot or observer acted as bomb aimer. This bombsight claimed an accuracy error of 30 yards from 6,000ft.

FE 2d A5 features the prominent external rectangular radiator, cut down pilot nacelle, single Lewis machine gun with retained cooling jacket atop one of three 'Anderson pillars' on the forward nacelle edge and 'fretted' lightening holes on the pilot seat.

When conducting photographic reconnaissance FE 2b/ds most often mounted a Thornton-Pickard type-C semi-automatic camera, whereby the glass plates were gravity fed via a handle that slid the plate into the camera from an upper magazine and then post-exposure removed it to a lower magazine. These cameras were mounted externally, often to starboard, and could be operated by the observer or the pilot, the latter via a rod and shutter cable that extended back to the rear cockpit, enabling the pilot to change plates and take photographs. FE 2s usually overflew the areas to be photographed and conducted several passes to ensure complete area coverage – this was when they were most vulnerable to sudden aerial attack. For oblique photography they employed cameras such as the 'special 23in. whole-plate camera', installed inside the front cockpit with the lens protruding through a panel in the side of the nacelle.

The stability of the FE 2 for such a role is exemplified by the recollection of Sgt James McCudden, future Major, VC recipient and 57-victory ace, who flew the FE 2 prior to switching to single-seat fighters:

The FE [2d], with the 250 [hp] Rolls [Royce engine], was a wonderful machine, and the way our observers and pilots used to climb round the capacious nacelle was most amusing. In fact, on patrol, up high, I sometimes stood on my seat and looked over [the wing at] the tail, the machine was so steady and stable. My observer never liked this part of the performance, especially when one day I was doing it and one of my gloves blew off into the propeller, which shed a blade, and very nearly wrecked the machine before I could reach my seat and throttle my engine down.

An FE 2b observer demonstrates the flexibility of his forward-mounted Mk II Lewis machine gun, with 97-round 'double drum' magazine. Body contortions were necessary for proper aiming. To the observer's left is a telescopic mounting attached to an 'Anderson arch', the top of which protrudes from the cockpit.

Overall the RAF FE 2 was a success. Born from necessity to overcome the then insurmountable challenge of firing a machine gun through a spinning propeller arc, pressed into roles beyond its battleplane conception and forced to remain in service and carry on in the face of newer and superior German aeroplanes, the FE 2 participated in some of the war's bloodiest conflicts – Verdun, the Somme, Arras and 'Bloody April' and Passchendaele. Outclassed though it was for much of it, the FE 2 was not merely fodder for German victory lists, as will be seen. It often gave as good as it got, and many German aviators ran foul of 'the big Vickers.'

Rear defence is demonstrated via a stock-equipped Lewis on a telescopic mount that is affixed to the 'Anderson arch'. Return fire above could be served in this manner but aggressive manoeuvring or a defensive circle was required to effectively remove the rear blind spot.

FE 2b/d COLOURS AND MARKINGS

Western Front FE 2b/ds employed PC10 (alternately referred to as Pigmented Cellulose Spec. No. 10 and Protective Colouring No. 10, which generally had a chocolate brown to greenish khaki appearance that varied with age and length of ultraviolet light exposure) nacelles, wings and empennage uppersurfaces, the latter of which 'wrapped around' the leading or trailing edges to encroach 1.5 to 2 inches on the clear-doped fabric undersurfaces. Early nacelles could remain natural metal or were painted battleship grey.

Although any nacelle could feature blue/white/red roundels, this was not universal, but roundels were always located on the uppersurfaces of the upper wings, either outboard near the tips or just inboard of the ailerons, and the undersurfaces of the lower wings. Rudders were evenly divided into blue/white/red bands (from leading to trailing edge), with serial numbers (which could be black, white, bordered, non-bordered or any combination) across the white and red bands.

Generally, RFC squadron markings were not used, or were quite subtle compared with German standards, and usually consisted of markings on the nacelle. For example, No. 11 Sqn employed a white 'hollow triangle' on the nose of the nacelle (said to be an unofficial marking, but photographs reveal it was employed nevertheless) and No. 25 Sqn a horizontal black line with white borders.

Many machines were 'presentation aircraft' donated by Commonwealth societies or individuals, and these machines were marked by the names of the contributors. For instance, *Zanzibar 1*, or *Presented by the Residents in the Punjab*. Personal markings were occasionally seen on nacelles, even on presentation machines, such as *The Scotch Express*, as were individual flight markings (e.g. 'C 6'), which might also have been applied to the upper wings.

FE 2b and FE 2d comparison specifications		
	FE 2b	FE 2d
Dimensions		
Wingspan	47ft 9in.	47ft 9in.
Chord	5ft 6in.	5ft 6in.
Dihedral	4.0 degrees	4.0 degrees
Length	32ft 3in. (tricycle undercarriage)	31ft 9in. (Trafford Jones)
Height	12ft 7in.	12ft 7in.
Armament	2 x Lewis Mk 1 0.303in. machine gun	2/3 x Lewis Mk 1 0.303in. machine gun
Weight (lb)		
Loaded Weight	2,967 (120hp Beardmore)	3,469 (250hp Rolls-Royce)
		3,037 (160hp Beardmore)
Performance		
Engine	120/160hp Beardmore	250hp Rolls-Royce
Maximum speed	80.5mph at sea level (120hp Beardmore)	94mph at 5,000ft
	91.5mph at sea level (160hp Beardmore)	
Climb to 10,000ft	51 min 45 sec (120hp Beardmore)	39 min 44 sec (160hp Beardmore)

ALBATROS D I – D V

The Albatros D-series was born from the need to counter the numerous Nieuport and DH 2 fighters that had arrested the German monoplane fighter superiority and turned the tide of the 'Fokker Scourge' by late spring 1916. The key to the Albatros's success was its Mercedes D III engine, a normally aspirated, direct-drive, water-cooled, carburetted, inline, overhead-cam, six-cylinder engine. Initially rated at 160Ps (a measure of horsepower [*Pferedestärke*, or Ps], where 1.0hp equals 1.014Ps), the Mercedes D III saw service with the Albatros D I, D II and D III. During the latter's production run the engine had its

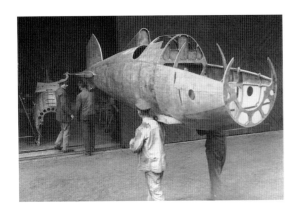

A framed and skinned Albatros D V fuselage is manhandled to the next production area for undercarriage installation. This view clearly illustrates the model's new, entirely ovoid, fuselage cross-section that required wing 'stub' attachment points. Note the large headrest.

A succinct example of machine gun synchronisation failure and its results, this on *Jasta* 11 pilot Karl Schaefer's Albatros D III 2062/16. Such damage would cause immediate and severe vibration and require throttling back or shutting down the engine.

pistons redesigned to increase power to 175Ps, and in this capacity was used through to the Albatros D V, before being superseded by the 180Ps Mercedes D IIIa, which was fitted into the D Va and D Va (OAW) production runs.

In all Albatros D-types, fuel and oil tanks were located immediately aft of the engine, all of which except the cylinders was cowled within detachable metal panels – there was no firewall. Pilot engine management included a control column-mounted throttle, a spark-retarding lever on the port cockpit wall, along with an engine magneto switch key (which was removable and attached to a chain that in some photographs is seen dangling outside of the cockpit) and starting magneto crank. Albatros engine starts did not employ ground personnel to 'swing' the propeller. Instead, the left engine magneto was switched on and the starting magneto hand-cranked from the cockpit, sending current to the spark plugs that caused a continuous spark discharge within the cylinders that ignited the fuel/air mixture and started the engine. There was also an auxiliary throttle control located port-forward in the cockpit.

Cooling for the D I and D II was provided by port and starboard Windhoff fuselage-mounted radiators located just forward of the cockpit, with a triangular expansion tank fitted above the engine and slightly to port of the longitudinal axis. One early pre-production and all late-production D IIs replaced the Windhoff radiators and expansion tank with a Teeves & Braun radiator that was centrally mounted within the upper wing and plumbed externally to carry coolant to and from the engine. Thereafter, this configuration was standard on all Albatros D-types, although during the middle of the first D III production batch the radiator was offset to starboard.

The Mercedes engine turned a fixed-pitch wooden propeller made of glued walnut and maple or walnut and ash laminations (import shortages of wood in 1916 also necessitated using teak, elm and pine), the hub of which was enclosed within a large aerodynamic spinner. Commonly used propeller manufacturers included Axial, Garuda, Reschke, Astra, Heine and Wolff.

The Albatros's firepower consisted of two fixed and forward-firing Maxim LMG 08/15 7.92mm air-cooled machine guns, each synchronised to fire 500 rounds through the propeller arc at a maximum rate of 450 rounds per minute. This rate was dependent upon engine speed, and varied greatly with different propeller rpms used by the synchronisation gear that compensated for the variable frequency with which the blades passed before the gun muzzles. Despite the availability of Fokker's two-gun synchronisation gear, Albatros chose instead to devise and utilise an in-house two-gun synchronisation mechanism designed by *Werkmeister* Hedtke and modified by *Werkmeister* Semmler (Albatros apparently tested Fokker's mechanism in October 1916, but deemed the test unsuccessful and remained committed to the Hedtke system).

Triggers were centrally located on the control column near the throttle and situated so that the guns could be fired separately or simultaneously, and the gun breeches were pilot accessible for cocking and clearing jams. Hemp-belted cartridges were stored in magazines forward of the cockpit and fed to the guns via curved metal chutes. After passing through the guns the empty belts descended separate chutes to collect in bins adjacent to the magazines – cartridge cases were ejected overboard. As with the engines, the breeches were partially cowled within detachable metal panels.

The semi-monocoque wooden fuselage employed six longerons to which was nailed a shellacked and varnished 2–3mm scarf-jointed, three-ply birch laminate skin. The D I through D III (OAW) fuselages employed an ovoid cross-section up to the leading edge of the wings that became vertically slab-sided back to the tip of the tail, although throughout its length its spine and belly retained their ovoid curves. The intersection of the curved belly and slab-sided fuselage at the lower wing leading and trailing edge connection points created drag-producing protuberances that required the installation of either wood or metal aerodynamic fairings.

From the D V on, the fuselage was redesigned with a fully ovoid cross section that eliminated the slab sides, easing construction and reducing the machine's form drag – wooden 'stubs' were provided for wing attachment points. All D-types employed a leather-coamed open cockpit in which the pilot sat in a high-sided, padded bucket-type seat, adjustable fore and aft, with a four-point seatbelt and shoulder harness restraint. Standard instrumentation consisted only of an engine tachometer, fuel valves and a floor-mounted compass, although altimeters and airspeed indicators were commonly installed in-field. A conventional rudder bar and control column enabled pilot control about the axes, although there were neither brakes nor trim, and a small windscreen provided some protection from the slipstream.

Albatros cockpits were more spacious and protective than those of many enemy aeroplanes, and without an engine firewall the Albatros pilot enjoyed the warming benefits of radiant engine heat that the crews of FE 2s did not.

Lift for the Albatros D I and D II was provided by two equal and constant chord, subtley tip-tapered wings of slightly unequal span, affixed to the aeroplane with positive stagger but without dihedral or sweepback. The upper wing was a one-piece structure that attached to the fuselage via inverted V-struts (similar to those employed on the Albatros C-types) that were slotted to permit fore or aft adjustment of stagger. Here, the D I and D II differed markedly, with the D I's inverted V-struts giving way to the D II's outwardly splayed N-struts and its wing gap reduced by lowering the upper wing 9.8in (250mm).

Both upper and lower wings featured dual spar construction with internally wire-braced plywood ribs enclosed within a skin of doped fabric (which pulled against the approximately 1mm diameter wire trailing edge to create the classic scalloped appearance). They were braced externally with wire rigging and streamlined steel struts, steel-tubed, fabric-covered ailerons. The latter, located on the port and starboard

This view of Albatros D III 2061/16 with its upper wings removed affords an unobstructed glimpse of its 160PS Mercedes D III engine and twin Maxim LMG 08/15 machine guns. The white rectangular placard displays rigging data for groundcrew, and the open hatch allowed visual inspection and carburettor access.

ALBATROS D FUSELAGE GUNS

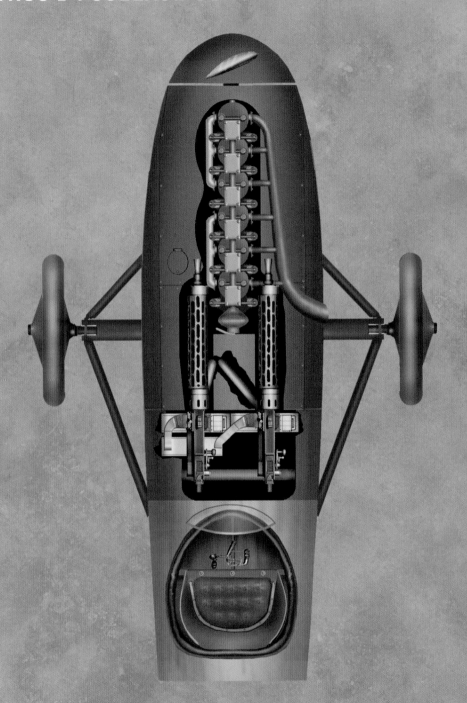

Albatros D-type scouts were armed with two fixed air-cooled Maxim IMG 08/15 machine guns synchronised to fire through the spinning propeller arc, each gun being belt-fed 500 7.92mm cartridges. Rate of fire was set at approximately 450 rounds per minute per gun, although engine RPMs altered this rate significantly to compensate for the variable frequency with which the propeller blades passed before the gun muzzles.

ALBATROS D III COCKPIT

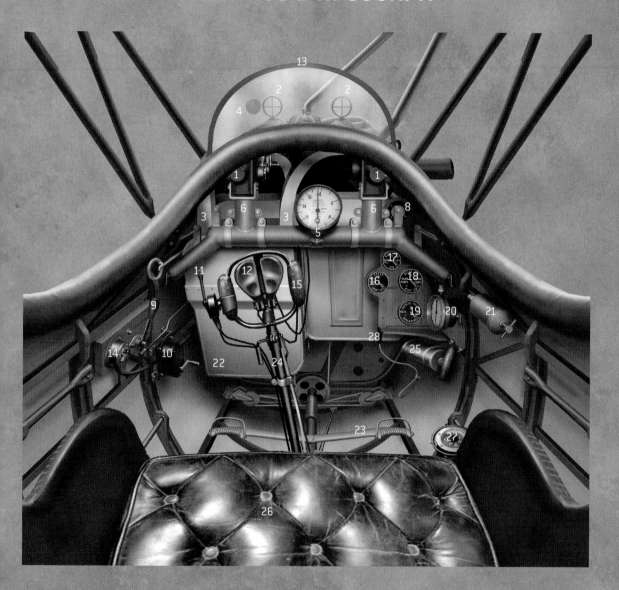

1. 7.92mm LMG 08/15 machine guns
2. Ring and bead gunsights
3. Ammunition chutes
4. Windscreen with hole at left to allow gunsighting if stained with oil
5. Tachometer
6. Machine gun rotating brackets
7. Auxiliary throttle handle
8. Fuel pressure gauge
9. Spark control handle
10. Starting magneto
11. Throttle handle
12. Machine gun buttons
13. Windscreen
14. Magneto switch key

15. Control column grip
16. Fuel tank pressure valve
17. Fuel pressure gauge valve
18. Air pump selector valve
19. Fuel tank flow selector valve
20. Fuel quantity gauge
21. Water pump greaser
22. Ammunition belt container in front of two ammunition cans
23. Rudder control bar
24. Control column
25. Hand-operated air pump
26. Adjustable leather-padded aluminium seat
27. Magnetic compass
28. Drain cock

Albatros D tail progression. Top, D III (same as the D I and D II rudder); middle, Albatros D III (OAW); and bottom, Albatros D V, which also featured a redesigned tailskid and under-fin area. Although said to be interchangeable, the OAW rudder often appears slightly more bulbous along its lower trailing edge than the D V's.

outboard upper wing trailing edges, provided lateral control about the aeroplane's longitudinal axis.

Beginning with the D III, the aeroplane was redesigned into a sesquiplane configuration, whereby the lower wings were of lesser chord than the upper, and built around a single spar. This required the fore and aft interplane struts to be connected to the dual upper spars and the single lower spar, resulting in the classic 'V-strut' configuration that the Albatros Ds retained thereafter.

This redesign had been influenced by flight testing of captured Nieuport fighters, and was purportedly introduced to increase manoeuvrability and downward visibility. However, as previously noted, the single spar construction introduced problems with structural integrity – lower wing failures – and led to temporary grounding, modification and redesign. The worst of the problem was overcome, but it was never eradicated.

The wood-framed empennage featured a ply-covered vertical stabiliser and two fabric-covered horizontal stabilisers, all of which employed curved leading edges and low aspect ratios. The steel-tube framed counter-balanced rudder and one-piece elevator were covered with doped fabric and operated via cables that fed through the fuselage and into the cockpit. D I through D III rudders had vertical trailing edges, while those from the D III (OAW) onwards had curved trailing edges. A one-piece steel-shoed ash tailskid supported the empennage, which was bungeed for a measure of shock absorption. Similarly, the main landing gear employed bungeed shock absorption that also served to connect the steel-tube V-struts to the wheel axle, and a steel restraining cable was used to limit axle travel and prevent gear collapse in the event of bungee failure.

Performance specifications for the various Albatros Ds were fairly consistent between the different models, despite a modern misconception that there was constant performance degradation with each new type. Weight had steadily increased from the D I – although it decreased initially with the D V – but that penalty was offset by the use of higher-powered engines and the reduced form drag of the more aerodynamically efficient ovoid fuselage cross-section of the D V/D Va (OAW). The result was that the new models flew with nearly universal performances – e.g, as reported by *Idflieg* in July 1917, 'the performance of both [Albatros D III and D V] is the same'.

The misconception about performance degradation largely evolved from the reports of British pilots flying captured German machines, who afterwards naturally compared Albatros flight characteristics with those of the more nimble RFC machines they were used to flying. Obviously, one's first and often only flight in an unfamiliar and foreign Albatros D V was not going to be as nimble an experience as flights often enjoyed in a familiar Sopwith Pup. However, such reports did not imply that the D Va performance was lacking compared with the D I.

However, what degraded over time was pilot attitude toward the Albatros. This was fostered by increasing dissatisfaction with each new model's performance commonality with the model it superseded, and structural problems with the wings introduced by the sesquiplane redesign of the D III. Meanwhile, Albatros pilots began facing new makes and models of RFC tractor fighters that had joined the older FE 2s aloft in increasing numbers – SPAD VII, Sopwith Pup, Sopwith Triplane, SE 5, SE 5a, DH 5, etc., with the Sopwith machines being especially well regarded for their manoeuvrability. When German pilots could not outmanoeuvre them whilst on the defensive, and diving away with superior speed could prove problematical due to the problems with sesquiplane structural integrity, it is understandable that frustration began creeping in around the edges.

In late September 1916, *Jagdstaffel* 2's Ltn Erwin Bohme wrote that he regarded the Albatros D I as 'marvellous', and 'far improved over the single-seaters we flew at Verdun [Eindeckers]', with a rate-of-climb and manoeuvrability that were 'astonishing'. However, less than a year later in July 1917, *Jagdgeschwader* Nr 1 *Kommandeur* Rittm Manfred von Richthofen wrote that the new Sopwith single-seaters 'played with' the Albatros D V, which he felt was 'outdated' and 'ridiculously inferior to the English single-seaters'. Still, in the hands of a capable fighter pilot – of which there was no dearth in the *Luftstreitkräfte* – as the series matured, the Albatros Ds remained useful and formidable weapons.

ALBATROS D I – D V COLOURS AND MARKINGS

Although produced by three different manufacturing companies (*Albatros Flugzeugwerke* and *Luftverkehrsgesellschaft* [LVG] of Johannisthal and *Ostdeutsche Albatros Werke* [OAW] of Schneidmühl) that employed camouflage variations, the Albatros D I – D Va (OAW) employed a high-gloss shellacked and varnished birch fuselage that has been described as appearing 'warm straw yellow' in colour. The spinner, engine cowling panels, fittings, access hatches, vents and cabane/interplane/undercarriage struts were either light grey, pale greenish-grey or greenish-beige. D I – D V wheel covers and undersurfaces of the wings, ailerons, horizontal stabilisers and elevator were a light blue, although the uppersurfaces and national markings varied between the individual manufacturers.

Johannisthal-built aeroplanes of the *Albatros Flugzeugwerke* had wing uppersurfaces painted in two-tone camouflage of Venetian red and olive green (D I) or three-tone camouflage of Venetian red, olive green and pale green (D II/III). The pattern of camouflage colours and their port or starboard directional slant varied between machines. Beginning with the D V, Albatros camouflaged their wing uppersurfaces in swatches of green and mauve, and eventually used printed (rather than painted) four- and five-colour irregular polygon fabric, with reportedly 'salmon'-coloured rib tape. The fabric-covered rudder could be either clear-doped linen or often one of the various camouflage colours, and starting with the D V could be clear-doped linen or printed four- or five-colour fabric – again, this varied between machines.

National markings consisted of a black *Eisernkreuz* on a square white crossfield at eight points – one at each upper and lower wingtip (although some lower wing crosses were applied directly to the blue undersurfaces without a white crossfield

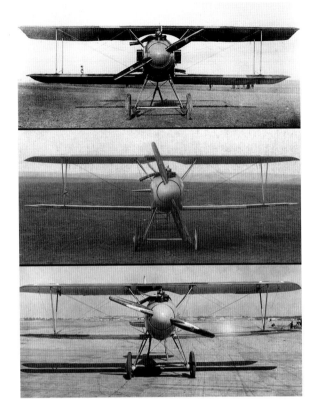

Albatros D fuselage progression. Top, the D II (same as the D I), prior to relocating the radiator to the upper wing on later D IIs; middle, D III, which had redesigned wings but retained the D I's slab-sided fuselage; and bottom, the D V, with a fully ovoid fuselage.

or border), one on each side of the fuselage, well aft near the horizontal stabiliser, and one each side of the tail, overlapping the hinge line of the vertical stabiliser and the rudder. Beginning with the latter D II production runs, this crossfield was eventually eliminated.

A black serial number, such as 'D.1177/17' (where 'D' represented the aircraft designation [single-engined single-seat biplane with armament], '1177' denoted it was the 178th machine of the first production batch [D.1000–1199/17] and '/17' was the last two digits of the year the machine was ordered), was hand-painted on either side of the vertical stabiliser. Thus, although similar, no two numbers were exactly alike.

Starting with the D III, a two- or three-line weights table was located beneath the cockpit and variably depicted empty weight, permissible weight with full fuel, payload and total weight. Manufacturer and *Idflieg* placards were located on either side of the nose and on the leading edge of the lower wings, just outboard of the interplane struts. Finally, an Albatros company logo (a helmeted bird with wings spread in flight) adorned each side of the rudder and was applied so that both port and starboard birds faced (i.e. 'flew toward') the spinner, although there were occasional exceptions.

Additionally, some D IIs had their fuselages camouflaged in bands of olive green and rust brown, with the fuselage bottom painted pale blue with a subtly-feathered and sometimes hard-edged demarcation between the upper and lower surfaces. Furthermore, other Albatros D II fuselages may have been stained reddish-brown and varnished, based on an *Idflieg* document stating 'experiments by the Albatros firm have proved that colouring the fuselage (plywood parts) is possible without an appreciable increase in the A.U. weight (50 grams)'.

OAW-built Albatros D IIs were finished similarly to their Johannisthal brethren – warm straw yellow fuselage, grey or greyish-beige metal fittings, with the wings and horizontal stabilisers/elevator finished in what has been described as 'patches of burnt sienna and light and dark green blending into one another' (although photographs reveal this 'blending' was often very course and rough) – with 'undersurfaces very pale blue'. However, other OAW machines had their fuselages entirely camouflaged in the same manner and colours as the wings, including the course blending, with their bellies light blue from nose cowl to tailskid. Engine panels remained a shade of grey.

Eisernkreuz national markings were located at the usual eight points, all of which bore a 5cm white border instead of a square crossfield, and the fuselage crosses were located further forward than those on the Johannisthal machines. Serial numbers were allocated to the wheel covers and spinner rather than the vertical stabiliser, and the fuselage manufacturer and *Idflieg* placards were located just below the cockpit.

The Albatros D II cockpit. The fuel control valves are located at right, beneath the Maxim support bar that displays a non-standard clock. The tachometer is obscured forward, while the control column and its triggers and throttle are clearly visible. Note the central rear view mirror, Maxim gun 'Beule' (bulge), external flare stowage and honeycombed radiator at left. The curved dark object at right is the exhaust manifold.

OAW D IIIs employed green and mauve camouflaged wings and horizontal stabiliser uppersurfaces, the colour demarcation of which was spanwise on the stabiliser, with pale blue undersurfaces. Later model OAW D IIIs and D Vas employed printed polygon fabric, with rib tape that was reportedly light blue in colour.

LVG-built D IIs shared the Albatros *Flugzeugwerke* machine's warm straw yellow fuselage with the standard greyish metal fittings – wing root fairings were often wood. Wings, horizontal stabiliser and elevator camouflage was distinctive in its appearance, with light and dark bands of burnt sienna, dark green and light Brunswick green that were diagonally mirrored on either side of the centre line. Wing undersurfaces have been described as 'pale greenish-blue' or 'duck egg green' and the rudder was normally one of the uppersurface camouflage colours. National markings were in the usual eight-point positions, initially on white crossfields, but these were later replaced by white-bordered crosses, although some machines displayed both types. Serial numbers were not seen on the vertical stabilisers, and a weights table was positioned low on the port fuselage, just above the lower wing. An LVG company logo (a star spangled blue pennant with gold LVG in the middle) adorned each side of the rudder, under the cross and adjacent the bottom hinge.

STAFFEL MARKINGS

The arrival of the D I and D II in the frontline in the autumn of 1916 coincided with the formation of the *Jagstaffeln*, but generally these machines were not overpainted in garish colours and markings to the degree the Germans employed by the following spring. However, various *Staffeln* did adorn their fighters with unit emblems, such as *Jasta* 23's swastika, while others based their markings on a 'theme', such as *Jasta* 2's abbreviated pilot names (although Ltn Manfred von Richthofen and Oblt Stefan Kirmaier preferred vertical stripes, and *Staffelführer* Hptm Oswald Boelcke used nothing at all). *Jasta* 5 went with individual letters, while geometric symbols were preferred by *Kampfstaffel* 11.

Individual markings were not unknown, such as *Jasta* 22 Josef Jacobs' *KOBES* or Prince Friedrich Karl's skull and crossbones, inspired by his prior service with the 'Death's Head Hussars' 1 (*Leib-Husarem-Regiment* Nr. 1). Entire fuselage overpainting was not unknown, either. Indeed, several *Jasta* 2 machines were overpainted green or brown (including the fighter flown by the Prince), although this practice was neither as common nor ostentatiously employed as would be seen during 1917, when overpainting became the norm.

Staffeln regularly employed unit colours, with pilots adding colours and markings not only for personal affectation, but in-air recognition. For example, *Jasta* 11 used red fuselages, struts and wheel covers for its unit marking, but individual markings were limited to different-coloured tails, spinners or fuselage bands and stripes. Intricate personal markings were generally not seen. Conversely, intricate markings were widespread amongst *Jasta* 5's D Vs, which, along with their *Staffel*-identifying green and red empennages, had personal markings that included faces, crests, geometric shapes, chequerboard patterns, animals, flowers, etc. In any unit, rarely was an Albatros seen in the field that was not adorned by some sort of colour or marking augmentation beyond the factory norm.

Albatros D I, D II and D III comparison specifications*			
Albatros	D I	D II	D III
Dimensions			
Wingspan (upper)	27ft 11in.	27ft 11in.	29ft 6in.
Wingspan (lower)	26ft 3in.	26ft 3in.	28ft 10in.
Chord (upper wing)	5ft 3in.	5ft 3in.	4ft 11in.
Chord (lower wing)	5ft 3in.	5ft 3in.	3ft 7.5in.
Length	24ft 3in.	24ft 3in.	24ft 0.5in.
Height	9ft 8in.	8ft 8in.	9ft 6in.
Armament	2 x 7.92mm IMG 08/15s	2 x 7.92mm IMG 08/15s	2 x 7.92mm IMG 08/15s
Weight (lb)			
Empty	1,530	1,484	1,484
Useful load	502	496	518
Loaded	2,032	1,980	2,002
Performance			
Engine	160Ps Mercedes D III	160Ps Mercedes D III	160Ps Mercedes D III
Maximum speed	109mph	109mph	109mph
Climb to 3,281ft	4 min	4 min	2 min 30 sec
Climb to 6,562ft	10 min	10 min	6 min
Climb to 9,843ft	19 min	19 min	11 min
Climb to 13,123ft	30 min	30 min	17 min

Albatros D III (OAW) and D V comparison specifications*		
Albatros	D III (OAW)	D V
Dimensions		
Wingspan (upper)	29ft 6in.	29ft 6in.
Wingspan (lower)	28ft 10in.	28ft 8in.
Chord (upper wing)	4ft 11in.	4ft 11in.
Chord (lower wing)	3ft 7.5in.	3ft 4in.
Length	24ft 0.5in.	24ft 2in.
Height	9ft 6in.	9ft 0in.
Armament	2 x 7.92mm IMG 08/15s	2 x 7.92mm IMG 08/15s
Weight (lb)		
Empty	1,463	1,500
Useful load	502	518
Loaded	1,965	2,018
Performance		
Engine	160Ps Mercedes D III	160/180Ps Mercedes D III
Maximum Speed	109mph	109mph
Climb to 3,281ft	–	4 min 20 sec
Climb to 6,562ft	–	8 min 20 sec
Climb to 9,843ft	–	14 min 30 sec
Climb to 13,123ft	–	22 min 40 sec

*Figures are source dependent and vary.

The Schneidemühl-built Albatros D III (OAW) largely resembled Johannisthal's D III externally – the most noticeable difference was its curved rudder – yet internally the fighter was more structurally sound. This meant that the aeroplane avoided the lower wing issues that plagued Johannisthal-built D IIIs and D Vs. (Reinhard Zankl)

THE STRATEGIC SITUATION

When Archduke Franz Ferdinand of Austria and his wife Sophie, Duchess of Hohenberg, were assassinated in Sarajevo on 28 June 1914, their deaths became the catalyst for events that begat World War I. National relations that were already strained soon crumbled, creating a domino effect as country after country mobilised its forces to honour pre-war treaties. In August, after a month of political demands and negotiations had failed to stymie the worsening situation, German troops invaded and overran Belgium and then pushed into France, nearly reaching Paris before French and British counterattacks finally halted their advance.

The opposing forces then established entrenched defensive positions that eventually spanned an area from the Swiss border to the North Sea, and the war's first weeks of offensive mobility gave way to the defensive static trench warfare of 'No Man's Land'. The war that was supposed to have been won by Christmas was now deadlocked, with no end in sight.

The first year of hostilities saw little change along these trenches except failed offensives and a mounting death toll. By the end of 1915, 1,292,000 French soldiers, 612,000 German soldiers, and 279,000 British soldiers had been killed or wounded (these figures are approximate as casualty figures vary). Any territorial advancement purchased by these casualties was measured in yards.

Frustrated by their inability to break the stalemate, German Chief of Staff Erich von Falkenhayn believed French capitulation could be wrought via overwhelming casualty. Toward that end he attacked the fortress city of Verdun on 21 February 1916, reasoning the French would defend it at all cost. Falkenhayn's plan was not so much to capture

Verdun but rather provoke the French into a series of counter-attacks during which they would be annihilated. However, scepticism exists regarding the authenticity of Falkenhayn's claim to 'bleed France white', this statement in fact being nothing more than after-the-fact justification in his memoirs, and not the keystone of his actual strategy.

Regardless, although final figures differ, the French indeed suffered appalling causalities as they held Verdun, with some 542,000 men killed or wounded. Yet they were not the only ones being bled white, as German losses were some 434,000 killed or wounded. Ironically, these casualties led to Falkenhayn being replaced by Gen Paul von Hindenburg, although his deputy, Gen Erich Ludendorff, exercised the real power and served as the *de facto* general chief of staff.

Aeroplanes played an important role during these battles, conducting reconnaissance crucial for armies to formulate strategy by providing strategists with real-time views of enemy forces far beyond the lines. Obviously the value of attaining an aerial reconnaissance advantage over one's enemy while denying him the same was so clear that both sides sought to prosecute the development of quick, single-seat 'scouts' for the purpose of two-seater reconnaissance interdiction and destruction.

Initially, these single-seaters were hamstrung by the problem of synchronising a forward-firing machine gun to shoot through a spinning propeller arc. The British side-stepped this by pursuing development of pusher-configured aeroplanes, eliminating any need for synchronisation. Contrastingly, Germany and France – with the latter at the forefront of pusher design and manufacture – had been working on synchronising machine gun fire since 1910. By 1914, French aeroplane manufacturer Morane-Saulnier had developed a synchroniser gear, but tests revealed bullets still occasionally struck the propeller. While addressing this problem, Raymond Saulnier devised the back-up solution of also installing steel wedges to the propeller to deflect bullets that would have otherwise shattered the wooden blades.

During this period, Dutchman Anthony Fokker had also been working on a means by which a fixed machine gun could be fired through a propeller arc via an interrupter gear. The latter is believed to have been based on a 1913 patent held by Franz Schneider, a Swiss with the German firm LVG, the gear preventing the weapon from firing whenever a propeller blade passed before the muzzle. Demonstrating this device at Doberitz a month after its capture and inspection (the gear had been fitted to a Morane-Saulnier monoplane that had been downed in April 1915), Fokker was awarded a contract to produce interrupter gear-equipped aeroplanes.

This new machine was the Fokker E I, a mid-wing monoplane powered by an air-cooled 80hp rotary engine. By mid 1915 German pilots were using this new weapon to attack reconnaissance aeroplanes, the Fokker scout's presence over the front ushering in a desperate period for the Allies during which Germany held tactical air superiority. Prior to the FE 2, the RFC had no effective machine with which to counter this threat, and necessarily changed its tactics to state that 'a machine proceeding on reconnaissance must be escorted by at least three other fighting machines, and a reconnaissance should not be continued if any machines become detached'. Four aeroplanes were now required to do the work of one.

As the horror of Verdun trudged through 1916, the French urged a British offensive to lessen France's military burden. As a result the British initiated the Battle of the Somme on 1 July. However, by this time the 'Fokker Scourge' had been countered

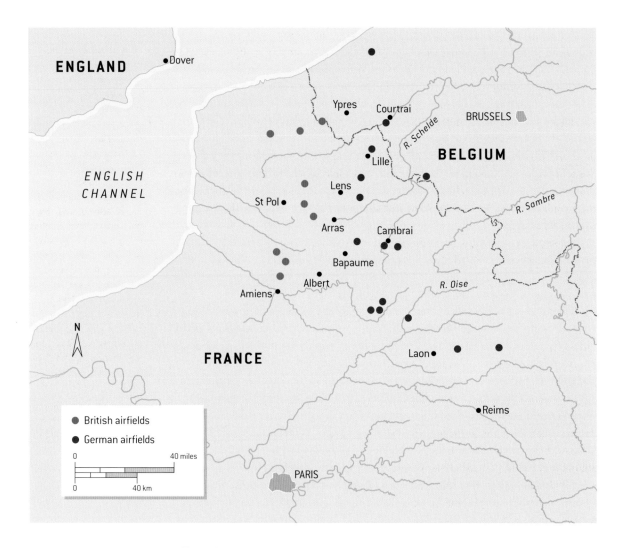

ENGLAND

•Dover

ENGLISH
CHANNEL

Ypres

Courtrai

R. Schelde

BRUSSELS

BELGIUM

Lille

Lens

St Pol •

Arras

Cambrai

R. Sambre

Bapaume

Albert

R. Oise

Amiens •

N

FRANCE

Laon •

Reims

● British airfields

● German airfields

0   40 miles

0   40 km

PARIS

effectively by the arrival of Allied single-seater fighters, namely the French Nieuports, and as the British and German armies slogged through yet another stygian bloodbath (British casualties on the first day of the Battle of the Somme alone were some 19,000 killed and 41,000 wounded) the RFC's FE 2 and DH 2 pushers were helping to dominate the skies above.

The arrival of German single-seat and single-gun biplane fighters could not alter the tide as the Somme battles flared on and off in a series of small attacks and counter-attacks, and on 15 September the British launched the battle of Flers-Courcelette, using tanks for the first time.

This offensive coincided with a restructuring of the German air force and the arrival of its first in-line engine, twin-gun fighters – the Albatros D I and D II – which left an immediate impression on their enemies. The British did not retreat from these machines, but they recognised that new aeroplane types of their own were needed to counter the technologically superior Albatros. As Commander-in-Chief of the British Expeditionary Force Sir Douglas Haig wrote at the end of September 1916, 'the enemy has made extraordinary efforts to increase the number, and develop the speed and power, of his fighting machines. He has unfortunately succeeded in doing so, and it is necessary to realise clearly, and at once, that we shall undoubtedly lose our superiority in the air if I am not provided at an early date with the improved means of retaining it'.

Haig found some reprieve as 1917 arrived and winter gripped Europe. Quite expectedly, combat operations slowed for both sides and afforded time for self-assessment and strategic planning. The Entente rejected a peace proposal tabled by the Central Powers that included the annexation of territories they currently occupied, and French dissatisfaction with Gen Joseph Joffre's inability to break the Western Front attrition led to his replacement by Gen Robert Nivelle. The latter had fought at Verdun, and he believed that the success of his artillery-based counterattacks there could be amplified and implemented along the entire front, thus dissolving the two-year deadlock.

To assist with his plan to 'break the enemy's front in such a manner that the rupture can be immediately exploited', Nivelle proposed that Haig's forces conduct preparatory attacks at Arras and Bapaume, with Cambrai as the main objective, to draw out German reserves. The French would then launch a major offensive in the Champagne that would employ intense artillery fire followed by massive infantry frontal attacks.

However, Gen Ludendorff recognised that Joffre's replacement by the attack-minded Nivelle meant an offensive was likely to arrive with the spring. Therefore, the German lines, which bulged into enemy territory between Arras and Riems, had to be fortified. Ludendorff duly established a line of defence at the base of this salient called the *Siegfriedstellung* (Seigfried Zone, or 'Hindenburg Line', as it was dubbed by the Allies), some points of which were 20 miles behind the original German trenches, and in February 1917 troops withdrew to this shorter and more readily defended line. The territory the Germans had previously occupied was abandoned to the Allies, although everything of value had been destroyed, mined, or booby-trapped as they went. This withdrawal was completed by 16 March, and it provided the Germans with a heavily fortified line that could be defended by fewer troops than before, with reserve forces positioned in such a way that they could quickly respond to an attack anywhere along the *Siegfriedstellung*.

Meanwhile, the German *Jagdstaffeln* had continued their organisation and expansion, and although the Albatros D II's presence was still strong, the new Albatros D III had started to arrive in ever-increasing numbers. Redesigned as a sesquiplane with a lower wing of reduced chord that initially suffered from serious structural integrity issues, the aircraft's problems had been rectified (although D III pilots knew not to prosecute a protracted dive lest they risk departure of a lower wing) by February. This allowed the *Jagdstaffeln* to attack the British reconnaissance two-seaters that were being continually sent across the lines to gather intelligence in support of the pending offensive.

The RFC still flew FE 2s on bombing, photo-reconnaissance and offensive patrols, but by now it was clear the pushers were well past their prime. New machines had been developed, such as the Bristol F 2A and RAF SE 5, but these would not trickle in until April. Thus, for the time being, Trenchard had no choice but make do with what he had.

The stage was now set for the German and Entente forces to engage in what has become known as 'Bloody April', particularly with regard to the aerial battles associated with the British Arras offensive that began on 9 April. Casualty figures vary,

OPPOSITE
The RFC FE 2 bases were of a more permanent nature than those used by the highly mobile *Jagdstaffeln*, which made prodigious use of tent hangars and travelled via rail along the frontline, hence their familiar sobriquet 'Flying Circus'. Although the sleek Albatros scouts outperformed their belligerent pusher counterparts, they were generally outnumbered, and thus the *Idflieg* usually concentrated its forces at key points close to the ground fighting. Offensive RFC tactics guaranteed that many machines would reach and cross the lines, so forward observers were employed by the Germans to monitor the airspace and telephone nearby *Staffeln* with contact information regarding an incoming enemy sortie, thus sending the *Jagdflieger* aloft in pursuit.

but more than 240 RFC machines are known to have been lost to either German aeroplanes or ground fire, with 300+ airmen killed, wounded or missing. Meanwhile, the ground offensives for which these men perished enjoyed initial success that quickly faded, and British forces were unable to prosecute their early gains in the face of strengthened German resistance.

Nivelle's 16 April offensive – employing more than one million men and 7,000 artillery pieces – suffered from lack of surprise, reduced intelligence from the high casualty rate of aerial reconnaissance aeroplanes and strong German counter artillery. Worse still, the French 'rolling barrage' that comprised a curtain of artillery fire ahead of and at the same speed as advancing troops had progressed too rapidly, subjecting the exposed soldiers to catastrophic German machine-gun fire. The French managed to capture the first German trench line before they were stopped, this 600 yard advance falling well short of Nivelle's expected six miles. In the first five days of the campaign Nivelle's units had had 120,000 men killed or wounded.

French soldiers viewed this offensive as a flagrant waste of human life, and by month-end the survivors began rebelling, refusing to attack any further and agreeing to fight only in defence of the French lines. News of rebellion resounded through the trenches, and soon the French army endured widespread mutiny. The entire fiasco led to Nivelle being relieved of command, by which point even reservists refused to go to the lines. By June 54 French divisions were mired in mutinies that new commander Gen Philippe Pétain assuaged in part by adopting a policy of 'aggressive defence', whereby further French offensives would be of limited and more realistic scope. He cleverly chose to bide his time until the Americans – who had declared war on Germany on 6 April 1917 – began arriving *en masse*.

As the French regrouped, Haig decided to proceed with plans for an offensive in Flanders. His desire was fuelled by the pre-war treaty obligations to protect Belgium and restore it to a sovereign and neutral state. In so doing British troops would overrun U-boat pens believed to be located along the coast at Ostend and Zeebrugge. On 7 June, after many days of preparatory artillery bombardment in what was to become the battle of Messines, 500 tons of fused explosives were detonated in mineshafts that for months British engineers had tunnelled under the German lines.

Bolstered by tanks and poison chlorine gas, the British advanced with a goal of capturing the high ground of the Messines–Wytschaete Ridge, which they did. However, this was but a planned diversion to take Passchendaele, and on 18 July more than 3,000 artillery pieces began firing 65,000 shells at the Germans, cratering 'No Man's Land' and reducing it to a 'virtually impassible morass' when combined with the worst rains in decades. The main attack began on 31 July, and for weeks the Allies pushed on, enduring mud, machine guns and mustard gas. In the skies above, airmen in FE 2s and Albatros D Vs swirled in their own morass of machine guns, defensive circles and long flaming deaths.

By the time Passchendaele Ridge and the nearby village was captured in November, to the tune of some 300,000 Allied and 260,000 German casualties, the FE 2 had flown off to pasture, while the next generation of Albatros, the D Va, had arrived in-country. Although dangerous in capable hands, it was not greeted with the same enthusiasm as would the Fokker D VII, although the latter type would not reach frontline units until the spring of 1918.

THE COMBATANTS

ROYAL FLYING CORPS

In 1915 the German deployment of the Fokker Eindecker and its synchronised machine gun caused such casualty and concern amongst British bombing and reconnaissance two-seater crews that by year-end the RFC notified its squadrons that 'until the Royal Flying Corps is in possession of a machine as good as or better than the German Fokker it seems that a change in tactics employed has become necessary. It is hoped very shortly to obtain a machine which will successfully engage the Fokkers at present in use by the Germans'. One change in tactics stated that 'a machine proceeding on reconnaissance must be escorted by at least three other fighting machines, and a reconnaissance should not be continued if any machines become attacked'.

Without reliable synchronisation gear of their own, British aeroplane manufacturers tended toward development of pusher aeroplanes with engines and propellers mounted behind the pilot, bypassing any need for machine gun synchronisation. Focusing on pusher configuration led to the development of the FE 2a/b/d, the Aircraft Manufacturing Company's single-seat DH 2 and the RAF's single-seat FE 8. Thereafter, reliable synchronisation had been developed and implemented by all sides, and thus British aeroplane manufacturers evolved beyond the pusher concept and focused on tractor-powered aeroplane designs instead.

By the end of 1915 even the pusher types already developed were still absent from France in significant numbers – only seven FE 2s were in service with the RFC (four FE 2as with No. 6 Sqn, and three FE 2bs with No. 16 Sqn).

In a view that highlights a juxtaposition of fragility and might, No. 20 Sqn FE 2d A6516 illustrates its varied capacities as a 'battleplane' (three Lewis machine guns, including one fixed for the pilot), bomber (underwing rails for bomb racks and a bombsight next to the pilot's cockpit) and photo-reconnaissance machine (observer's camera).

One of the first FE 2as in France in 1915 was 4227, assigned to No. 6 Sqn and flown by future RFC luminary Lanoe Hawker – he would be best remembered for his exceptional leadership when commanding No. 24 Sqn and an epic final dogfight with 'Red Baron' Manfred von Richthofen in November 1916. In August 1915 Hawker was flying 4227 when he was attacked by a 'very fast scout monoplane which tried to get behind the F.E. – I turned the F.E. very sharp and succeeded in facing it. The scout crossed about 50 yards in front, firing at us'. Hawker's observer, Lt Clifton, wrote that Hawker out-turned the monoplane, who then 'straightened out, by luck right in front of us, and even I couldn't miss him'. After 'some steady shooting at 50 yards' the German aeroplane 'suddenly turned nose straight down and fell away at a terrific speed'. This was credited as Hawker's sixth, and penultimate, victory.

While the FE 2 demonstrated it could more than hold its own against the cutting-edge technology of a synchronised fixed machine gun fired through a spinning propeller of an attacking aeroplane, there just were not enough of them. Finally, in late January 1916, No. 20 Sqn arrived in France with 12 FE 2bs. By May, Nos. 18, 22, 23 and 25 Sqns had bolstered the FE 2's ranks to more than 60 machines. Whereas before the RFC had to marshal its resources redundantly (three escorts for each reconnaissance machine) in a defensive strategy to counter the 'Fokker Scourge', the FE 2b battleplanes helped swing the RFC's mindset from defensive to offensive.

From that point the RFC's offensive spirit never wavered, even after the arrival of Germany's new Albatros D-type scouts in September 1916, the impact of which was immediately noted by Commander-in-Chief of the British Expeditionary Force, Sir Douglas Haig, who wrote in a letter to the War Office on 30 September 1916 that 'the enemy has made extraordinary efforts to increase the number, and develop the speed and power, of his fighting machines. He has unfortunately succeeded in doing so, and it is necessary to realise clearly, and at once, that we shall undoubtedly lose our superiority in the air if I am not provided at an early date with the improved means of retaining it'.

Meanwhile, FE 2s shouldered a wealth of responsibility for bringing the fight to the enemy and assumed various roles, including photo-reconnaissance, escort, daylight bombing, night bombing and offensive patrols as battleplanes. Despite inferior performance compared with the Albatros scouts, the FE 2s attacked, attacked and attacked again. They did not merely fight back but actively sought and initiated combat, often giving as good as they got (likely wounding Germany's leading ace Manfred von Richthofen and knocking him out of the war for five months just prior to Third Battle of Ypres) and even more so (killing von Richthofen protégé and *Jasta* 28 Kommandeur Karl Emil Schaefer, whose 30 total victories contained seven FE 2s). As von Richthofen wrote in his Air Combat Operations Manual, 'a long aerial combat with a completely combat-ready, manoeuvrable two-seater is the most difficult'.

LUFTSTREITKRÄFTE

Aerial combat in World War I was not a fair fight. It was never intended to be. Neither side had any interest in mere parity – they were up to their eyebrows in parity along the trenched edges of 'No Man's Land'. What they sought was superiority. Yet, superiority was a large pendulum with an arc governed by technological advances.

When the war began both sides were relatively even with regard to aerial threats upon one another, but upon the implementation of aeroplanes manufactured with machine guns synchronised to fire between the spinning blades of a rotating propeller, the pendulum clearly swung in Germany's favour when the Fokker Eindeckers carried their 'scourge' into history. Even though they did not down Allied combat machines by the gross during this period, the successes they had caused a reformation of British strategy to focus on redundant protection, in essence greatly reducing the size and influence of the RFC as a whole.

When the RFC pushers arrived in 1916, the pendulum began its swing back the other way. By the time legendary German ace Max Immelmann was killed in combat on 18 June while flying a Fokker E III against FE 2bs, air superiority was fully under British control – and French control as well, since the latter's Nieuports with their over-wing machine guns also had a large hand in arresting the 'Fokker Scourge'. Shortly thereafter German interest and demand for inline fighters capable of carrying one or even two machine guns surfaced, and by 1916 Albatros had designed and produced prototype examples of what would become one of the war's most iconic and successful single-seat fighters, the Albatros D-series. Although, similar to the FE 2's production delays, Albatros production languished throughout that summer as inline engine allocation priority favoured two-seaters.

Albatros D V 2004/17 at Johannisthal. Note the gap between the spinner and the engine cowl that permitted cooling air to enter the engine compartment, and that the undercarriage shock absorbing bungees were housed within protective sheaths.

MANFRED VON RICHTHOFEN

Known globally today as 'The Red Baron', Manfred Albrecht *Freiherr* von Richthofen was born on 2 May 1892 in Breslau, Silesia, Germany. He and his two brothers and sister grew up in nearby Schweidnitz (today Swidnica, Poland), where as a child young Manfred spent much of his time hunting. At his father's behest he entered military academy in 1903, attending Walhlstatt until 1909 and Lichterfelde until 1911. In school von Richthofen excelled in sports and equestrian activities, but less so scholastically, later confessing he 'did just enough work to pass'. Upon graduation he was assigned to the 1st *Uhlan* Regiment.

Following the commencement of World War I von Richthofen served as a cavalryman on the Eastern and Western fronts, but when the initial war of mobility morphed into one of static trench warfare, he found himself mired there in boredom, running messages and attending telephones instead of leading cavalry attacks. This led to his request and ultimate transfer into the *Fliegertruppe* as an observer, in which role von Richthofen felt his training as a cavalryman would serve him well. He served for several months in that capacity, and with time an interest in shooting down enemy aeroplanes waxed within – despite several aerial encounters he had no success. However, a chance meeting with Germany's most successful fighter pilot, Oswald Boelcke, inspired von Richthofen to learn to fly because he reasoned that the difference in their levels of success was that Boelcke 'flew a Fokker fighter, and I a large battleplane. Thus, I decided, "You must learn to fly a Fokker yourself, then perhaps things will be better"'.

Thereafter, he began informal flight training between his normal observer sorties, attaining his pilot's certificate on Christmas Day, 1915. Through the summer of 1916 von Richthofen flew two-seater reconnaissance and bombing sorties on both fronts, and eventually rigged a machine gun to an LFG Roland C II and shot down a Nieuport scout, although this victory was unconfirmed and is therefore not part of his credited victory list. Fortunately, while flying in Russia, he again crossed paths with Boelcke and was chosen among others to join the great ace's new *Jagdstaffel* 2, in France. It was a sage choice. Less than three weeks after his arrival he shot down his first confirmed aeroplane – an FE 2b – during his first combat sortie in a new Albatros D I. This was his first of 13 eventual FE 2b/ds victories, and the first of some 56 victories he would attain flying an Albatros single-seater.

Initially enthusiastic about the new, fast, well-armed D I, as time passed von Richthofen's enthusiasm waned with the arrival of improved British aeroplanes and Albatros's failure to deliver expected and desired performance enhancements with subsequent models. In July 1917, after experiencing essentially the same performance with the new Albatros D V as he had with preceding models, von Richthofen had had enough – especially after being wounded in one. On the 18th he wrote a letter in which he referred to the Albatros as 'lousy', and that 'the [Sopwith] triplane and the 200 [hp] SPAD as well as the Sopwith single-seater [Pup] play with our [Albatros] D V', which he opined was 'outdated and ridiculously inferior' to the RFC machines it faced. Regardless, von Richthofen shot down four more aeroplanes flying an Albatros D V, until after an extended recuperative leave he returned to fly Fokker Dr I triplanes – the type in which he was shot down and killed by small arms fire on 21 April 1918.

F. J. H. THAYRE AND F. R. CUBBON

Frederick James Harry Thayre (above) was born in London on 20 October 1894. He initially flew BE 2s with No. 16 Sqn in 1916 and attained his first victory on 18 March when his observer shot down an attacking Fokker E III. After transferring to No. 20 Sqn, Thayre teamed up with Francis Richard Cubbon (right), who was born in London on 26 November 1892, but had resided in Poona, India, before the war. Cubbon had served with the 72nd Punjabis and then the Royal Warwickshire Regiment before being seconded to the RFC in October 1916, and in April 1917 he had paired up with Thayre in No. 20 Sqn to become what would be the most successful FE 2 team of the war.

Flying FE 2d A6430 *AJMER*, the pair opened their victory tally by flaming two Albatros D IIIs on 29 April, and the following month were credited with 15 victories, 13 of which were Albatros D IIIs. During a bombing sortie on 3 May No. 20 Sqn was 'attacked by about 26 Albatros Scouts led by [a] machine painted entirely red. FE A6430 engaged 18 at once. Two he [A6430] crashed, one at 5.20pm and one at 5.25pm. FE A6430 then ran out of ammunition, and as there were still three HA [Hun Aircraft] he attacked with an automatic revolver [sic], driving the three HA away'. On 23 May the pair crossed the lines in A6430 and 'attacked about nine Albatros Scouts. One HA got on our tail and we turned and fired both guns forward, and he went down with

the right hand side wings hanging off and was lost in a bank of clouds'. Together Thayre and Cubbon shared 19 Albatros D III and two Albatros C-type victories, with personal victories tallying 20 and 21, respectively.

Their meteoric streak ended on 9 June 1917 when, on a bombing sortie to Comines, 'A6430 dived at a two-seater and drove it down in a vertical nose dive, with smoke coming out [the fate of this German aeroplane is unknown, and Thayre and Cubbon did not receive victory credit]. FE A6430 was then hit apparently by AA fire, went down and did not return'. The RFC Combat Casualties reported the 'death of Capt F. J. H. Thayre accepted by the Army Council as having occurred on 9/6/17 on the evidence of a message dropped from a German aeroplane', which specified that both Thayre and Cubbon had been killed. Despite their post-mortem identification, the men have no known graves. Both were awarded the Military Cross and Bar for 'conspicous gallantry and devotion to duty'. Thayre was noted for 'coolness and courage enabling his small command to inflict severe losses on numerically superior forces', while Cubbon was cited for 'displaying great skill and courage against superior numbers of the enemy. Throughout the action he backed up his pilot with a remarkable display of marksmanship'.

However, this delay turned out to be serendipitous, for the first Albatros production D Is began arriving in France just as the German *Fliegertruppe* had reconstructed into the *Luftstreitkräfte*. On 8 October 1916 Gen Ltn Ernst von Hoeppner was promoted to *Kommandierenden General der Luftstreitkräfte* (*Kogenluft*), which in turn made him answerable to the Chief of the General Staff of the Armies in the Field for the use of all German air forces at the front, and for training and unit formation at home. This included all flying formations in the field, army airships at the front, the Meteorological service, the *Flugabwehrkanonen* (*Flak*) and the organisation of the aerial defence of Germany.

Much of this reorganisation was born from lessons learned at Verdun and the Somme that had demonstrated the importance of single-seater aeroplanes in the destruction of enemy aircraft. When the *Luftstreitkräfte* realised that an increase in the number of two-seaters would not yield air superiority over the front, priority was placed on the continued development of single-seat fighters. By August 1916 all available single-seaters were concentrated in pursuit squadrons called *Jagdstaffeln* (Hunting Squadrons, or *Jastas*). This organisation of single-seaters allowed them to be based at decisive points along the front, and they were to assume the primary role in the quest for aerial supremacy.

That was the might. The sharpest lance that might wielded was the Albatros D I, even though initially its impact was not experienced across the breadth of the entire front. After all, there were only 50 D Is manufactured, and it took until the end of October for all of them to reach the front, where they were joined by 28 D IIs that had begun trickling in – the first of more than 200 that would arrive by year-end. As Gen Ltn Ernest von Hoeppner recalled in his memoirs:

> The expeditious equipment of all the pursuit squadrons with aeroplanes capable of the proper performance was a further necessity. We were behind [the enemy] in this respect. It had been demonstrated that our Fokkers were inferior to the new hostile pursuit aeroplanes in both speed and ability to climb. During the Battle of the Somme they were replaced by new pursuit types. The Halberstadt and Albatros factories succeeded in building some single-seater biplanes that were swift and good at climbing. These were termed D aeroplanes. The strength of their armament (they were equipped with two fixed and coordinated machine guns [the Halberstadt Ds had only a single machine gun]) was to have made up for our lack of numerical superiority.
>
> The organisation of single-seater aeroplanes into pursuit squadrons [*Jagdstaffeln*] made it possible to concentrate them at decisive points on the battlefield – it also made it possible to exercise a personal influence on their training and employment. The number of pursuit aeroplanes and their technical performance, together with the leadership and valour of their pilots, were, from now on, to assume the first role in aerial combat and the struggle for air supremacy.
>
> But numbers alone are no guarantee of success. The aeroplane itself is a lifeless thing unless the pilot inspires it with his coolness under fire and his unfaltering desire to attack. Therefore, the selection of pilots for assignment to pursuit squadrons had to be made with the greatest care. Only those whose flying ability had been established by service with detachments that had been in action were to be chosen for training as pursuit pilots.

Ample were the opportunities to put such training to the test.

COMBAT

The many duels between FE 2s and Albatros scouts began upon the frontline arrival of the new Albatros D I scout in 1916, which coincided with Germany's premier ace Oswald Boelcke forming *Jagdstaffel* 2.

A new and permanent unit type, *Jagdstaffeln* were born from the reformation of temporary *Kampfeinsitzer-Kommandos* (KeK, or fighting single-seater commands) that were dedicated to aerial interdiction following their equipment with single-seater scouts. Yet for weeks *Jasta* 2 was burdened with just a smattering of Fokker and Halberstadt D machines, rather than a full complement of Albatros's new twin-gunned fighter, although Offz Stv Leopold Reimann arrived from *Jasta* 1 in late August and brought one of the new pre-production Albatros D Is with him.

Boelcke used this meagre 'fleet' for training during the first half of September, but on the 16th – the day *Jasta* 2 finally received its first allotment of Albatros D Is, as well as its D II prototype for Boelcke – he led some of his pilots aloft. At 1800 hrs Ltn Otto Höhne shot down his and *Jasta* 2's first FE 2b (6999 of No. 11 Sqn).

On 17 September, World War I's future ranking ace Manfred von Richthofen opened his 80-victory tally by shooting down another No. 11 Sqn FE 2b, 7018. Full of determination but void of experience in attacking 'the big Vickers', as the Germans called FE 2s, von Richthofen wrote that he exchanged shots with 7018's observer, Lt Tom Rees, but both men missed. This exchange likely comprised high-deflection shots, for Rees could only fire high behind the FE 2 (to clear the wings, tail, struts and propeller).

With a dose of right rudder, *Jasta* 2's Ltn Otto Höhne guns Albatros D I 390/16 *Hö* on its takeoff run during the autumn of 1916. On 16 September Höhne shot down No. 11 Sqn FE 2b 6999, which became the *Staffel's* first 'Fee' victory.

This machine is said to be No. 11 Sqn FE 2b 7018, which was shot down by Manfred von Richthofen for his first victory on 16 September 1916. The attack damaged the aeroplane's 160hp Beardmore engine and mortally wounded the crew, although pilot Lionel Morris lived long enough to safely land the machine.

Manfred von Richthofen subsequently wrote that after this opening gunfire he 'tried to get behind him' – i.e., he was not yet there – 'because I could only shoot in the direction I was flying [while an FE 2] observer's rotating machine gun could reach all sides'. Although 7018 'twisted and turned', von Richthofen managed to get behind the aeroplane when it flew straight and level (for reasons unknown, but it seems likely von Richthofen approached from the FE 2's blind spot at 'six o'clock low' and the crew just lost sight of him) and fired a burst from ten metres that hit the engine and stopped the propeller.

In his autobiography *Der Rote Kampfflieger*, von Richthofen wrote that he believed the crew had been injured, and he saw Rees's machine gun 'pointed unattended in the air', but his combat report reveals 'the machine went down gliding, and I followed until I had killed the observer, who had not stopped shooting until the last moment'. *When* Rees and his pilot 2Lt Lionel Morris were shot is irrelevant to the outcome. 7018 was going down regardless of their wounds, which killed Rees in the air and fatally injured Morris, who hung on long enough to successfully land the damaged machine. This engagement graphically demonstrated von Richthofen's 'no quarter' *modus operandi* that was not fostered with time but had existed from the beginning.

This no-quarter attack methodology was seen with von Richthofen's sixth FE 2 victory and 18th overall. Now commanding *Jasta* 11 and flying a new Albatros D III, he attacked No. 25 Sqn FE 2b 6997 and 'after a long fight I forced my adversary to land near Vimy'. The British crew survived the encounter, but their post-war recollections reveal the 'long fight' occurred after von Richthofen's first attack had shot through the fuel and oil tanks, damaged the propeller and disabled the engine. Thereafter the machine was gliding, but now aware of the FE 2b's blind spot, von Richthofen persistently 'attacked each time from below and behind, in which position we were unable to return fire'.

The sad remains of No. 20 Sqn FE 2d A27, shot down during a photo-reconnaissance mission over Lille and Messines on 17 March 1917. It was the first of eight victories credited to Fw Wilhelm Hippert. (Greg VanWyngarden)

This FE 2 rear blind spot and defensive-fire dead zone was an Achilles' heel, but to survive crews had to learn to adapt and overcome. As No. 20 Sqn observer Lt William Cambray – who was eventually credited with six aerial victories that included two Albatros D IIIs (the first of which was an Albatros D III while flying as observer for Capt Donald Cunnell, who, as will be seen, was involved in the war's most famous FE 2/Albatros duels) and three Albatros D Vs – explained:

The usual perch for the observer was on the side of the cockpit, always on the watch above and to the rear. The enemy usually collected a formation of six, then perhaps an additional eight, and when there were about 20 of theirs to five of ours they would come in close to attack. I would fire a red Very light, which told our formation we were going to fight. We would then go round and round in a big circle, each pilot following the tail of the man in front, and always making the whole circle approach gradually closer to our own lines. Should a Hun dive to attack, the observer of one machine in the circle would fire his top gun and the observer of the next FE would use his front gun so that at any given time the attacker would have two guns firing at him.'

The shattered and broken-boned corpse of 25-year-old ace Karl Schaefer lies amongst the smashed wreckage of his Albatros D III. The aeroplane had been brought down by a burst of machine gun fire from FE 2d A6469, the German scout going into a vertical and at least partially wingless dive until it hit the ground. Note that neither the wreckage nor Schaefer's clothes show any signs of fire. (Lance Bronnenkant)

But the FE 2s did not solely engage in reactionary, defensive combat with Albatros scouts. Along with photographic missions, they were employed as offensive weapons, often bombing targets and then actively seeking enemy aeroplanes to attack, the ability of which was augmented in June when No. 20 Sqn outfitted its FE 2ds with a third fixed and forward-firing Lewis machine gun for the pilot, increasing firepower by 50 per cent.

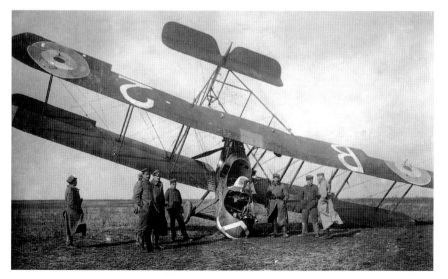

No. 11 Sqn FE 2b 7961 after being downed by *Jasta* 11's Ltn Kurt Wolff for his fifth victory on 31 March 1917. Attacked during a photo-reconnaissance sortie, 7691's engine and fuel tank were shot up and its observer, 2Lt William Clifton, mortally wounded. Pilot Lt Leslie Strange managed to bring the aeroplane down, after which he become a PoW. (Greg VanWyngarden)

On 5 June patrolling No. 20 Sqn FE 2ds were intercepted by 'about 14 HA', one of which was a 'red scout' flown by 30-victory ace and *Jasta* 28 *Kommandeur* Ltn Karl-Emil Schaefer. With his Albatros D III he attacked FE 2d A6384, sending it diving earthward (its mortally wounded pilot, Lt W. W. Sawden, made an emergency landing near Ypres) with Schaefer following. Lt H. L. Satchell and 2Lt T Lewis, in A6469, then dived after the German ace, with whom they entered a 15-minute battle until a 'long burst of fire at very close range' hit Schaefer's D III. The Albatros duly broke up in midair (accounts vary as to whether the aeroplane lost all or some of its wings, and if there was fire, although Schaefer's corpse and aeroplane wreckage appear to have been unburnt) and crashed vertically near Becelaere.

That same day, Capt Frederick Thayre and Capt Francis Cubbon of No. 20 Sqn shot down an Albatros D III. This proved to be their penultimate success of an incredible 19-victory streak that had commenced just six weeks earlier on 29 April. That day, No. 20 Sqn FE 2ds had dropped 20lb Cooper bombs onto the Bisseghem dump from 8,000ft, after which they were 'attacked on all sides' by '18 or 20 Albatros scouts of various colours'. Flying FE 2d A6430, Thayre and Cubbon had their oil tank, radiator and main fuel tank shot through, but after switching to the auxiliary tank they fought on and 'drove a machine down in a spinning nose-dive [east] of Menin, and the observer saw flames issuing from him'. They then 'drove down [another D III] in the same condition', which they said they observed crash. Afterwards they turned to attack four aeroplanes on their tail, but without result, and ultimately made a forced landing at Bailleul aerodrome due to their battle damage.

This action set the tone for the following month, during which Thayre and Cubbon were credited with 15 victories flying A6430, 13 of which were Albatros D IIIs.

Kurt Wolff, photographed in the spring of 1917, relaxes before a wall of serial numbers taken from his various victories, including the starboard serial number of 7691. Other souvenirs include the serial number from Bristol F 2A A-3338, the SFA number (3469) from Nieuport 17 B1511, a flare gun and plaque-mounted manufacture placards. A portrait of Manfred von Richthofen adorns the table.

Werner Voss suits up next to his famously painted, first-production batch Albatros D III. Voss tied with Walter Göttsch and Karl Schaefer for second behind von Richthofen for top Albatros 'FE 2 killer' honours, downing seven of his nine FE 2 victories while flying an Albatros D. (DEHLA Collection)

Combat reports reveal No. 20 Sqn was always outnumbered by Albatros scouts, yet never failed to engage them no matter how long the odds. Such was the case on 5 May, when the unit's FE 2ds were attacked by 'about 26 Albatross [sic] scouts'. In the subsequent action Thayre and Cubbon were credited with shooting down three Albatros D IIIs, after which they 'had completely run out of ammunition'. Yet a hand-written addendum to their combat report reveals that after exhausting their supply of ammunition they still attacked 'three HA' and drove them off with fire from their automatic pistols!

Several days later the pair bombed 'small houses around a major factory' near Ypres, but increasing anti-aircraft (AA) fire caused A6430 to 'come down in a spiral nose dive and sideslip from 12,000ft to 5,000ft. AA fire stopped, thinking machine was hit. Capt Thayre at once dived at the trenches, getting a drum of ammunition into them'. On 13 May they fought 12 Albatros scouts, which they kept at bay by firing over the upper wing and tail, but after attacking a scout they were set upon by four others, one of which they shot down. They were attacked again by three more and once again claimed a victory. On 25 May Thayre and Cubbon crossed the lines and were attacked by 'about nine Albatros scouts. One HA got on our tail and we turned and fired both guns forward, and he went down with the righthand side wings hanging off and was lost in a bank of clouds'.

Always willing to slug it out with the Albatros, and able to outfox flak gunners with deception, Thayre and Cubbon were, eventually, brought down by AA on 9 June. Flying A6340, they had dived at and driven down a two-seater aeroplane that they had left in a vertical, smoking nosedive. Moments later their FE 2d endured a direct flak hit and crashed, killing Thayre and Cubbon. The Germans subsequently dropped a message informing the RFC of their deaths, but the final resting places of Thayre and Cubbon remain unknown.

Less than a month later, Albatros D Vs of *Jasta* 11 became embroiled in a 40-minute battle with FE 2ds of No. 20 Sqn near Comines, in France, during which *Jagdgeschwader* Nr. 1 *Kommandeur* Manfred von Richthofen was wounded and forced to land to seek medical attention. The events and aftermath of this encounter have been perennially misunderstood, and require a very detailed examination of the war's quickest yet most famous FE 2 versus Albatros duel.

In the nine months since von Richthofen had been a neophyte fighter pilot with *Jasta* 2 (he had shot down one of the very first FE 2bs), he had blossomed into an enormously effective leader and Germany's top ace. As such, he was the obvious choice to lead *Jagdgeschwader* (JG) Nr. 1, a new organisation that assimilated *Jastas* 4, 6, 10 and 11 into a cohesive unit. Although von Richthofen oversaw *Geschwader* operations, he usually flew as part of *Jasta* 11, the unit with which he had flown and commanded since January, and his personal aeroplanes remained adorned with *Jasta* 11's red nose/struts/wheel cover identification colour. By July, von Richthofen was flying at least two different Albatros D Vs. Both had *Jasta* 11 colours, although personal markings differed between one aeroplane's red nose, tail and wings and the other's red wings, tail and fuselage.

At about 1030hrs (German time, one hour ahead of British time) on Friday, 6 July 1917, JG 1 received an alert of incoming infantry support aeroplanes that sent *Jasta* 11 aloft. Led by von Richthofen, *Jasta* 11 flew for the better part of an hour between Ypres and Armentières without enemy contact until they spotted FE 2s from No. 20 Sqn approaching the lines. These six machines were commanded by four-victory pilot Capt Donald Charles Cunnell, and they had departed St Marie Cappel, in France, between 0950hrs and 0955hrs for an Offensive Patrol above Comines, Warneton and Frelinghien, along the French/Belgian border.

Under orders to attack any enemy aircraft they encountered – a task about which none of the 12 men held any illusions, despite many successes, since dozens of previous sorties had demonstrated how German fighters could outmanoeuvre their two-seater pushers and 'shoot hell out of us from that blind spot under our tails'. Indeed, Cunnell's observer/gunner, 2Lt Albert Edward Woodbridge, opined that the FE 2s were like 'butterflies sent out to insult eagles. We were "cold meat", and most of us knew it'.

Dutifully they sallied across the lines to bomb an oft-targeted ammunition dump in Houthem, before reaching their assigned patrol area. Shadowing 'the Big Vickers' as they went, von Richthofen was content to bide his time and let them fly deeper into German territory. However, Cunnell's manoeuvring prior to No. 20 Sqn's bombing run fooled von Richthofen into believing that the English had detected *Jasta* 11 and were turning away to avoid combat. To counter this, von Richthofen led his Albatrosses south towards the FE 2s so as to position them west of the English formation and 'cut off their retreat'. By doing this he hoped that the presumably timid pushers would have no choice but to engage the Germans blocking their way back to St Marie Cappel.

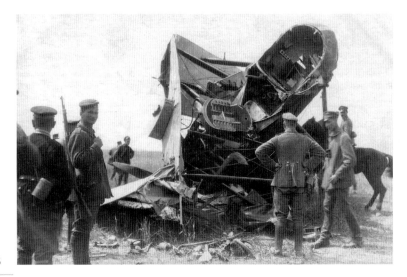

The smashed remains of this downed FE 2d illustrate the violence of terrain impact and the likelihood of crew injury or death – especially for the unrestrained observer. Note the shuttered radiator, exhaust manifold, control column and lightening holes in the pilot seatback.

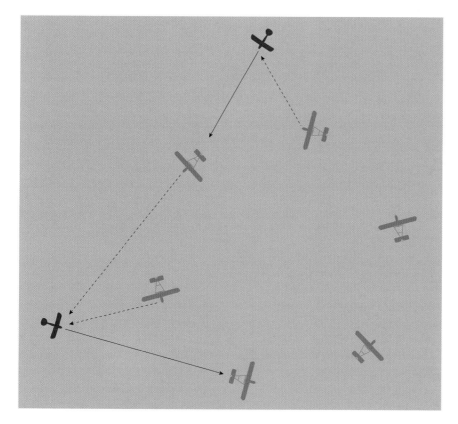

Unique to FE 2 crews was their use of a defensive circle. Employed in the face of overwhelming numbers, the aeroplanes would begin circling each other so that the following machines could effectively cover the tails of the preceding machines. This eliminated the FE 2's large, rearward blind spot and enabled multiple guns to be trained on an incoming fighter, with security that one's own aeroplane was being similarly defended. The FE 2s adjusted for wind to circle toward their lines, and operated in this manner until the enemy disengaged.

Moments after bombing Houthem No. 20 Sqn saw the Albatrosses behind them, approaching from the north and 'making for lines West of FE formation'. Anything but timid, Cunnell immediately banked right and led the pushers 'behind EA so as to engage them' – the butterflies were now chasing the eagles! – yet this chase had hardly begun when an estimated 30 additional Albatrosses swarmed in 'from all sides, also from above and below'. Within seconds, No. 20 Sqn had gone from quarry to hunter to becoming so tactically disadvantaged that it had little recourse but to form a defensive circle, as witnessed on the ground by Air Defence Officer Ltn d R Hans Schröder, who later wrote:

> Eight [sic] FEs were revolving round one another in couples. The technique and tactics of the English were amazing, their main principle being that each machine should not look after itself but its partner. Each one therefore protected the other against any attack by their German opponents.
>
> The Englishmen refused to be rushed, and their steadiness gave them an absolute superiority. Meanwhile, our machines tried to break their formation by a series of advances and retreats, like dogs attacking a hedgehog. They pirouetted and spiralled, but their movements exposed them to more risks than their opponents, who appeared to be invulnerable and unassailable.

Far from invulnerable, the FE 2s were in the middle of all they could handle. In A6512, Woodbridge fired continually, switching between the fore and aft machine guns as Cunnell 'ducked dives from above and missed head-on collisions by bare

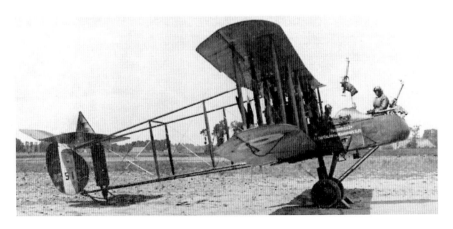

margins of feet'. He had never seen so many aeroplanes at once, and claimed a 'flamer' after firing 'a whole drum into him'. Cunnell claimed another two Albatrosses after firing 'large bursts from back gun' that 'entered [each] fuselage under pilot's seat', and A6498 observer 2Lt A. E. Wear's spirited fire led to a claim of 'one EA out of control' after 'a large burst at a range of about 20 yards entered EA from underneath, entering between engine and pilot'. Yet Woodbridge said the Germans 'went to it hammer and tongs' and inevitably their fire found its mark. A6376 had its oil tank and epicyclic gear shot through, A1963 suffered a damaged magneto and severed tail boom and observer 2Lt S. F. Trotter was mortally wounded defending A6419.

Aboard 6512, as Cunnell banked through 'the damnedest scrimmage imaginable', Woodbridge spotted two approaching Albatrosses – the first of which was an 'all-red scout'. This was von Richthofen, whose Albatros was in fact only partially red, but its red wings, struts and nose perhaps created an all-red appearance when observed head-on.

At some point after passing behind the FE 2s of No. 20 Sqn, he had reversed course and then led *Jasta* 11 back east toward the melee. Singling out A6512 – which von Richthofen later referred as 'the last aeroplane', suggesting the FE 2s' defensive circle had widened considerably and become ragged, or had even disintegrated altogether – he flew in from far enough astern to provide himself with ample time to 'consider a means of attacking.' However, he was unable to gain firing position before the FE 2

A somewhat grainy shot of the oft-photographed No. 20 Sqn A6516, which was configured like FE 2d A6512 that von Richthofen engaged in a head-on duel on 6 July 1917.

turned back at him in a head-on run – a tactical situation he disliked because 'one almost never makes the two-seater incapable of fighting' when attacking it head-on – and then commenced firing at him from an estimated range of 300 metres.

Yet von Richthofen did not disengage. Instead, he checked his fire and bore-sighted the FE 2, planning to pass beneath it before hauling his Albatros around to attack from 'six o'clock low'. He ignored Cunnell and Woodbridge's continuous gunfire as he came in, confident that 'at a distance of 300 metres [984ft] and more, the best marksmanship is helpless. One does not hit one's target at such a distance'.

Nevertheless, '300 metres' marked the beginning of A6512's gunfire, not the end, and therefore defines the length of the head-on run, during which the two aeroplanes converged at nearly 79 metres (260ft) per second at a combined speed of approximately 281km/h (175mph). Thus, two seconds after von Richthofen saw A6512 open fire the combatants had already covered more than half the distance between them. One second later, the 300-metre range had dwindled to 63 metres (207ft) – 72 per cent less than it had been just two seconds previously – and approximately half a second after that only 19 metres (60ft) separated the aeroplanes.

Woodbridge recalled that he and Cunnell 'kept a steady stream of lead pouring into the nose of that machine' as the aeroplanes converged, and he saw his own fire 'splashing along the barrels of his Spandaus [colloquial term for the Maxim machine gun]'. Return fire struck the cockpit around Woodbridge, yet von Richthofen recalls neither firing on the FE 2 (he later wrote that he had 'not even prepared my guns for firing') nor his Albatros taking any hits. Moreover, for 6512's head-on fire to have hit von Richthofen's guns would require the bullets to pass between the blades of his spinning propeller first, and post-battle photographs reveal these blades were free of damage. The multi-year, international quest for reliable machine gun synchronisation casts extreme doubt upon such long odds.

The Albatros D V that von Richthofen hastily landed in a field of thistles in Comines, France. Leading edge tape dangles from the lower port wing, and the machine's listing, tail-low appearance reveals tailskid and undercarriage damage – symptomatic of a hard landing. Note that the fighter's Garuda propeller is free of any bullet holes.

MARK POSTLETHWAITE '13

PREVIOUS SPREAD
On 6 July 1917, JG 1 *Kommandeur* Manfred von Richthofen discovered and shadowed a flight of No. 20 Sqn FE 2ds as they crossed the lines during an offensive patrol near Comines. After first bombing an ammunition dump in Houthem, the British machines spotted the Albatros Ds manoeuvring between them and the frontlines, and immediately turned to give chase, only to be attacked by many German machines that came in 'from all sides, also from above and below'. In the words of FE 2d A6512 observer 2Lt Woodbridge, this led to 'the damnedest scrimmage imagineable'.

Some minutes passed before *Jasta* 11 slowly entered the whirling fray, and von Richthofen had time enough to select 'the last machine' and 'consider a means of attacking'. This was A6512. But like the rest of the British pushers, it had had its dander up for several minutes by then and quickly spotted the German ace closing behind. Pilot Capt Donald Cunnell turned to face the attacker, and both he and Woodbridge opened fire on von Richthofen from about 300 metres, closing head on. Unconcerned by this long-range gunnery, von Richthofen held his own fire and planned to pass below the FE 2 and then come around and attack from its 'six o'clock low' – a direction from which the pusher could not return fire. Within seconds the two aeroplanes converged, but just before von Richthofen passed below A6512 a single bullet struck and caromed off the left rear side of his skull. Temporarily blinded and paralysed by the blow, von Richthofen was at the mercy of his out-of-control Albatros until he regained his faculties and conducted a successful off-field landing, after which he was hospitalised, grounded, and ultimately ordered

In any event, at some point during the 3.5- to 4-second head-on run – von Richthofen's recollection suggests early on, while Woodbridge's suggests towards the end – a single bullet struck the left rear side of the German ace's head and caromed off his skull, immediately rendering him both blind and paralysed. Dazed, his limbs fell uselessly from the controls and his Albatros hurtled underneath the FE 2 before rolling into a spiral dive. Cunnell immediately banked the pusher to thwart an expected stern attack, but instead he and Woodbridge watched as von Richthofen's aeroplane 'turned over and over and round and round. It was no manoeuvre. He was completely out of control'.

Inside the Albatros, the wounded but still-conscious von Richthofen felt his machine falling but could do nothing. His 'arms [hung] down limply beside me' and his 'legs [flopped] loosely beyond my control'. The engine noise seemed very distant, and it occurred to him that 'this is how it feels when one is shot down to his death'. Realising the increasing airspeed would eventually tear off the wings, he resigned himself to the inevitable.

Within moments, however, he regained use of his extremities and seized the flight controls. Killing the engine, he tore away his goggles and forced his eyes open, willing to himself, 'I must see – I must – I must see'. It was useless. Without vision, and likely experiencing some degree of spatial disorientation, he could not control the falling Albatros. Apparently it began a phugoid motion, whereby the aeroplane's diving airspeed increased lift and caused it to climb, which then decayed airspeed and lift until it nosed over into another dive to repeat the motion. 'From time to time', von Richthofen recalled, 'my machine had caught itself, but only to slip off again'.

After falling an estimated 2,000–3,000 metres, von Richthofen's vision returned – first as black and white spots, and then with increased normality. Initially it seemed as if he was 'looking through thick black goggles', but he soon saw well enough to regain spatial orientation and recover the Albatros from its unusual attitude. After recognising that he was over friendly territory, he established a normal glide east, and as he descended he was relieved to see two of his *Jasta* 11 comrades providing protective escort. Yet at a height of just 50 metres he could not find a suitable landing field amongst the cratered earth below, forcing him to restart his engine and continue east along the southern side of the Lys River until waning consciousness forced the issue, cratered earth or no. He had to get down immediately.

Fortunately, he had flown far enough east to spot a field free of shell holes, and he brought the Albatros in, flying through some telephone lines before landing in a field of tall floodplain grasses and thistles in far northeast Comines, in France. This location is confirmed via a post-landing photograph in which the 14th-century church Sint Medarduskerk is visible through the Albatros' starboard wing gap. Located on the northern Lys River bank in Wervik, Belgium, Sint Medarduskerk's orientation with respect to the photographed Albatros, corroborated by the author's personal reconnoitre of the area, verifies that the landing sight was indeed in Comines.

Where he landed made little difference to von Richthofen – afterwards, he could not even remember the location. Falling to the ground, he lay amongst the thistle until witnesses rushed to his aid. Amongst them was Hans Schröder, who had observed the entire action. When an ambulance arrived von Richthofen was placed in it and then driven to 16 Infantry Division *Feldlazarett* 76 in St Nicholas's Hospital, Courtrai.

His diagnosis upon admittance was 'ricochet to the head from machine gun bullet', the location of which was on the left side of his head, 'on the border between the occiput and the parietal bone'. Although the bullet was a non-penetrating ricochet, it created what doctors noted as a 'Mark-sized' scalp wound with slightly grey, irregular margins. Although there was 'no sign of internal bleeding or of an injury to the inner surface of the bone', von Richthofen, not surprisingly, complained of a headache. After medical personnel shaved his head and administered clorethyl anesthesia, Obergeneralarzt Prof. Dr Kraske operated to determine the nature and severity of the wound:

> On the base of the wound is still some musculature with periosteum [dense fibrous membrane covering bone surfaces, except at the joints, and serving as a muscle and tendon attachment] and galea [sheet-like fibrous membrane that connects the occipitofrontal muscle to form the epicranium {membrane covering the skull}]. Incision [is] to the bone. The bone shows only superficial roughness, no other injury. The cranium is not opened, and there is no sign of injury to its contents. Then the entire wound is excised within healthy tissue. Fairly strong bleeding. Several catgut sutures through the galea, skin sutures with silk.

Dr Kraske sutured von Richthofen's wound as completely as possible, but a portion three centimetres long by two centimetres wide remained open, exposing von Richthofen's bare skull. The wound was dressed with an iodoform gauze tamponade and a pressure bandage, and then his entire head above the ears was swaddled in bandages. He also received a tetanus shot.

On 25 July, after having felt well since 21 July, doctors deemed further hospitalisation unnecessary. The wound had changed little, although they noted a slight increase in granulation tissue, indicating healing. The still-exposed bone was covered with antiseptic boric acid ointment (in the era before penicillin, lethal infection was a significant concern) and the entire wound was covered with black ointment made from beeswax, herbs and oils, used to draw foreign debris from wounds and promote quicker healing.

Consulting surgeon Oberstabsarzt Prof. Dr Läven advised von Richthofen not to fly until the wound had healed completely, because 'there is no doubt that there was a strong concussion of the brain [commotion cerebri] associated with the wounding, even more likely, associated with an internal bleed. Therefore, it could happen during a flight, that the sudden changes in air pressure could cause disturbances of consciousness'. This contradicted the earlier diagnosis upon admittance that von Richthofen showed 'no sign of internal bleeding'. Regardless, having been informed of

away on recuperative leave. Although the wounding of von Richthofen was historically credited to Cunnell and Woodbridge, in the mid-1990s historian Ed Ferko postulated that 'friendly fire' from behind is what actually downed him. This begat careful scrutiny and cross-referencing of combat reports, personal anecdotes, photographs and gunshot wound analysis, and revealed that, despite his ultimately close proximity to A6512, von Richthofen was shot from neither the front nor the rear, but from either 'four o'clock high' or 'ten o'clock low'.

Mark Postlethwaite's rendition of the 6 July action portrays the latter possibility, and depicts the moment after von Richthofen was shot – in this case by an FE 2 that had been hidden under his lower port wing during his head-on closure with A6512. The reader is advised that this is but one of several possibilities regarding the origin of the wounding gunfire. The precise identity and location of the triggerman have been lost to time.

Manfred von Richthofen's fur-lined flight helmet worn on 6 July 1917. Although the helmet is flattened here, and thus somewhat misshapen, the bullet tear is clearly located above and behind the left ear flap and parallels a vertical seam extending up toward the top of the helmet.

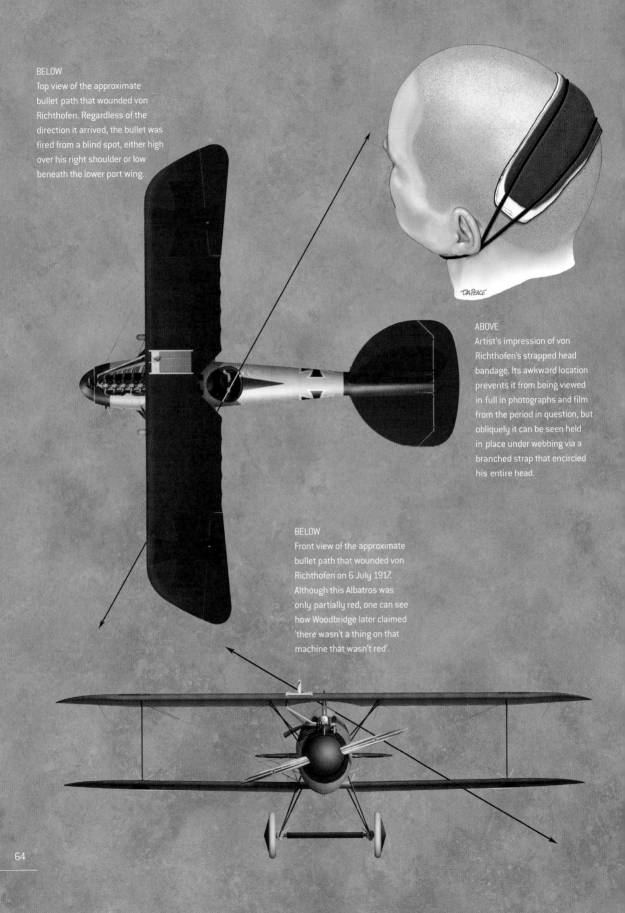

BELOW
Top view of the approximate bullet path that wounded von Richthofen. Regardless of the direction it arrived, the bullet was fired from a blind spot, either high over his right shoulder or low beneath the lower port wing.

ABOVE
Artist's impression of von Richthofen's strapped head bandage. Its awkward location prevents it from being viewed in full in photographs and film from the period in question, but obliquely it can be seen held in place under webbing via a branched strap that encircled his entire head.

BELOW
Front view of the approximate bullet path that wounded von Richthofen on 6 July 1917. Although this Albatros was only partially red, one can see how Woodbridge later claimed 'there wasn't a thing on that machine that wasn't red'.

this possibility, von Richthofen promised not to fly until he received medical permission – a promise that he soon broke (and one may speculate he never meant) – and shortly thereafter he was discharged.

Although history has long-credited Woodbridge with firing the wounding shot – for some reason Cunnell is never given credit, even though Woodbridge reported he fired as well – a theory exists that von Richthofen was actually hit by German 'friendly fire' emanating behind him. This theory is supported by the belief that when Cunnell and Woodbridge opened fire at 300 metres the distance was too great for accurate gunnery. The wound's rearward location also excludes the possibility of a frontal shot – i.e., how could an aeroplane in front of von Richthofen shoot him in the back of the head?

Prior to any conclusions regarding who shot von Richthofen, where he was shot must be determined, and direct evidence is lacking. There are no known photographs of the wound, and the head x-rays were destroyed in the 1970s to create storage room for modern records. Thus, the closest direct evidence comes via von Richthofen's medical history, whereupon hospital admittance surgeons described the wound as being located 'left on the border between the occiput and the parietal bone'.

'Border' refers to a suture, which is a line of junction or an immovable joint between the bones of the skull, where the bones are held together tightly by fibrous tissue. Specifically, the description refers to the Lamboid suture between the left parietal bone (one of two large bones which form the sides and top of the skull) and the occipital bone (the curved, trapezoidal bone that forms the lower rear skull). This suture runs at a 120-degree angle off the Sagittal suture, which runs front to back directly up the centre of the skull between the parietal bones. For a person sitting upright, the Lamboid suture runs downward from back to front at a 30-degree angle to the horizontal.

Despite that specificity, each skull is different. Some skulls have squat occipital bones while others are quite high, depending upon general skull shape. Therefore, the suture line between the occipital and parietal bones does not necessarily identify the same location on every person, but it does support the general assertion that when laterally viewing the left side of von Richthofen's head the wound was right of an imaginary line drawn vertically through the left ear.

This location is corroborated circumstantially via photographs taken of von Richthofen after his initial head 'swaddling' was removed sometime between 20 and 31 August (possibly the 27th, after bone splinters were removed from the wound) and replaced by a smaller, more localised dressing. Unfortunately, in most photographs the dressing is all but obscured by von Richthofen's flight helmet or other head cover, yet in at least two photographs and one cine film these obscurations are absent, affording a clear view of the dressing and its restraining chinstrap.

Beginning above and slightly behind the left earlobe, it ran vertically up and then across the top of the head to approximately as far right of the sagittal suture as the right eye – in a photograph in which von Richthofen faces the camera, the edge is at approximately '11 o'clock'. It was secured via a strap that wrapped under von Richthofen's chin and then up just behind the left earlobe, where it branched into two near-vertical and parallel straps connected via webbing (similar to a slingshot pouch) that continued across the top of the dressing to secure it. On the far side the parallel straps rejoined into a single strap above his right ear that descended vertically just in front of the earlobe, before passing back under the chin, thereby encircling von Richthofen's entire head.

The localised strapped gunshot bandage worn by von Richthofen is seen to good effect in this very late August or early September 1917 view from *Jasta* 11's quarters at Castle de Bethune, in Marckebeke, Belgium. Unquestionably, the bandage is oriented on Richthofen's head in the same location and vertical manner as his bullet-torn flight helmet.

It has to be presumed that von Richthofen was either shot frontally by A6512 or from the rear by another Albatros, and that he was focused on the onrushing FE 2 to avoid a head-on collision and judge his planned course reversal (i.e. sitting normally and looking forward – there would be little to no reason for him to look elsewhere during those scant 3.5 to 4 seconds). Knowing that bullets that create tangential wounds have a shallow impact angle with an almost parallel convergence between the bullet and the surface it strikes, von Richthofen's bullet wound should have been oriented more or less horizontally along the left side of his head, with at least some part of this wound crossing the Lamboid suture.

However, at least two reasons render a horizontal wound orientation unlikely. The first is von Richthofen's strapped-on localised dressing, which via the photographs and cine film noted previously was unquestionably aligned vertically rather than horizontally. Every doctor consulted agreed that using a vertical bandage the size of von Richthofen's would have been inconsistent with dressing a 10cm horizontally oriented wound because the ends of the laceration would have remained exposed. Rather, dressing a vertical wound entirely with a vertical dressing would have protected the still healing wound from dirt, sweat, the rabbit fur-lined flight helmet and the cold temperatures at altitude. It would have covered any pustules and incisions associated with bone splinters, and their removal, and it would have kept any topical ointments free of dirt and other septic impurities. Partially dressing a horizontal wound with a vertical dressing provides either no such protection or partial protection at best.

The second is a photograph of von Richthofen's flight helmet worn on 6 July that clearly shows a wide, jagged tear beginning (or ending) above and behind the left ear flap that parallels a vertical seam extending up toward the top of the helmet. On either side of this tear the helmet is undamaged – strong documentary evidence supporting vertical bullet travel.

Based on evidence, von Richthofen's wound was oriented vertically rather than horizontally, more or less parallel and slightly forward of the Lamboid suture, over which the 'mark-sized' wound initially gaped so that surgeons could see it. As noted previously, since bullets which cause tangential gunshot wounds traverse these wounds lengthwise along their long axes, then the bullet which inflicted von Richthofen's vertically oriented wound must have been traveling vertically as well. Therefore, he was shot from neither the front nor the rear.

Unfortunately, determining the bullet's exact origin and impact angle is impossible, as is determining the precise angle at which any bullet strike ceases to be a ricochet and instead becomes penetrating. There are far too many variables (speed, direction, trajectory, range, air pressure, air temperature, head movement, biological composition, projectile speed at impact, tumbling and intermediate barriers) to identify an absolute angular demarcation between ricochet and penetration.

Until the availability of wound ballistics studies which concern headshot ricochet angles, absolutes do not apply beyond the general principle that the flatter the impact angle the greater the likelihood of a non-penetrating ricochet. Additionally, although it is known that bullets which produce tangential gunshot wounds traverse these wounds lengthwise, it is difficult to establish direction – i.e., from left to right or right to left – without direct wound examination for *skin tags*. These are created when an impacting bullet stretches the skin until its elasticity is overcome and the margins of the resultant wound trough are multiply lacerated with the formation of these 'tags', or tears. The lacerated borders of these tags are located on the side of the skin projection nearer the weapon – i.e., they point in the direction the bullet travelled.

Without such precise directional evidence there are two possibilities. Since the Lamboid suture angles downward approximately 30 degrees from horizontal and forward approximately 30 degrees from vertical, then to inflict a tangential gunshot wound along this suture after a nearly parallel convergence and subsequently shallow impact angle, the bullet that struck von Richthofen must have arrived from either 'ten o'clock' and approximately 30 degrees below the Albatros's lateral axis (directly in the blind spot created by the lower port wing), or from 'four o'clock' and approximately 30 degrees above the Albatros's lateral axis – outside von Richthofen's peripheral field of vision.

Allowing for possible head rotation 45 degrees left and right of centre does not affect the 30-degree impact angles, but it would expand the azimuth slightly from 'ten' and 'four o'clock' to ranges of 'nine' to 'eleven o'clock low' and 'three' to 'five o'clock high'. However, von Richthofen was endeavouring to avoid a head-on collision, which meant that he was most likely sitting upright and facing forward to view A6512 when he was struck by the bullet.

Who fired this bullet, if neither A6512 nor an Albatros behind von Richthofen? The short answer – it likely will never be determined. The long answer – there are two possibilities:

1. Von Richthofen was shot by another Albatros. Friendly fire still cannot be discounted, considering the type of whirling battle described by Cunnell, Woodbridge and Schröder. It is not unreasonable to postulate, for instance, that an unseen Albatros tracked A6512 from the latter's 'four o'clock low' and opened fire from this position as the FE 2 began its head-on firing run at von Richthofen. A recalling Woodbridge stated that he and Cunnell came under fire at this time ('lead came whistling past my head and rip[ped] holes in the bathtub' [euphemism for the FE 2's fuselage]) but he presumed it was from von Richthofen. Such a deflection shot would require the unseen Albatros pilot to have continuously adjusted aim ahead of the FE 2 – perhaps one of its bullets struck von Richthofen when he suddenly appeared from the right and flew into this line of fire.

Of course, this illustrative speculation is but one of many possibilities. It is just as likely von Richthofen flew into bullets fired by the Albatros above him, which had aimed at another FE 2. The rounds missed the RFC aeroplane and struck von Richthofen instead. The possibilities are as many as one can conjure.

2. Von Richthofen was shot by an FE 2d other than A6512. It is possible he came under fire from several FE 2s at once, especially if they were still in a defensive circle. No. 20 Sqn's combat reports note 'several EA were engaged from favourable positions and at close ranges and driven down'. They also recounted how A6498 'brought down one EA out of control, firing a large burst at a range of about 20 yards, and tracers entered EA from underneath, entering between engine and pilot'. None of these

Fully suited for flight, an FE 2 observer demonstrates offensive gunnery. With uncompromised forward vision coupled with a flexible field-of-fire, the observer could easily fire down upon and wound the leading German ace as he passed by the FE 2.

claims can be linked to von Richthofen, but they do illustrate the frequency of multiple close-range firing encounters.

Despite the possibilities suggested by this work's presented evidence, there is no definitive answer as to who shot von Richthofen 6 July 1917, during the war's most famous FE 2 vs Albatros duel. Although gunshot wound ballistics exclude Woodbridge and Cunnell (regardless of their point-blank gunnery) as well as any German pilot flying with or directly behind von Richthofen, none of the various combatants' timelines and altitudes match well enough to state conclusively who fired the telling shot. That is, not beyond the generality that von Richthofen was struck by either an errant shot fired by another Albatros or a deliberate shot fired by an FE 2 in his blind spot. Either is just as likely, but across the decades any definitive answer has vanished into historical vapour – if it could have ever been determined at all.

STATISTICS AND ANALYSIS

The careers of the FE 2 and Albatros scouts paralleled one another in several regards. Both had close ties to the seminal origins of their respective air forces. Both were designed to overcome onboard weapon limitations – the FE 2's pusher design allowed the use of forward-firing machine guns without need for synchronisation gear to fire through a spinning propeller arc, and the Albatros's use of a 160hp engine allowed it to double the firepower of previous German single-seat scouts. Both aeroplanes helped foster a period of tactical superiority when they entered the war, and both were pressed into service beyond their glory days, although in capable hands they both continued to perform sterling service.

Despite these similarities, the Albatros scouts had several advantages over the FE 2. They were faster and their performance was better. However, the FE 2 could be manoeuvred quite aggressively for an aeroplane of its size. They usually outnumbered the FE 2 formations they attacked. Barring any jams, they fired two guns at once, which did not need reloading after every 47 or 97 shots, as did the FE 2's Lewis. And, with the RFC's offensive

Contrasting its ungainly and draggy design, the FE 2 had a somewhat sinister appearance of danger. This distant view illustrates the observer's enormous forward field-of-fire, as well as the blind spot aft and below.

strategy and daily behind-the-lines incursions, Albatros scouts more often than not fought FE 2s above German territory.

This was beneficial in several regards. First, they were not under constant exposure to AA fire. Albatros flight times were usually far less than an FE 2's, which often lasted 2.5 hours or more, prolonging crew exposure to cold and increasing the risk of hypoxia. *Jagdstaffeln* gathered near active areas of the front, with pilots suited for flight and stationed on alert near their fighters, waiting for forward spotters to telephone when enemy aeroplanes had been observed. Only then would they take off.

FE 2 crews operated from more permanent bases, had further to fly to the front and bombed targets well behind the front. They then often had to endure headwinds on egress, which reduced groundspeed and kept them over hostile territory longer, prolonging their exposure to aerial attack and AA fire. If gliding with a damaged engine, headwinds often prevented FE 2s from reaching friendly territory. If forced to land when battle-damaged, FE 2 crews were captured with their aeroplanes, unless they managed to burn them before German troops arrived. Either way, it could be unpleasant, as related by No. 11 Sqn's 2Lt Frederick Libby:

An Albatros D II struts its stuff, the aft elevator revealing that the pilot intends to go past the vertical and loop the machine. Of climbing Albatrosses, RFC ace James McCudden opined they 'gave the impression of a small dog begging'.

To be shot down and captured by the German Air Corps is not too bad, but to come down close to the lines where German infantry can get their hands on you is curtains. They shoot you quick and find a reason later. This is [because] the RFC often give the infantry a bad time by emptying their machine guns in the trenches on the way home, peppering the boys down there and often dropping a few 20lb bombs just for practice. Since the RFC are always [flying in] back of the German lines, the drill is that if one of our aeroplanes is out of commission and can't make it across our lines they are supposed to glide as far away from the trenches as possible, hoping to be picked up by the German Air Corps.

Since most fighting was over German territory, British claims were sometimes higher than shown by post-war research because it was easier for Germans to confirm their victories by visiting crash locations within their own lines. For a time the RFC counted as victories those enemy aeroplanes seen descending in a manner that appeared to be 'out of control' (OOC), but without a requirement of crash eyewitness. For example, during the battle in which Cunnell and Woodbridge fought Manfred von Richthofen on 6 July 1917, they not only claimed his Albatros D V but also three others all as OOC. Similarly, also present in that battle just after von Richthofen went down was 10 Naval Squadron pilot Raymond Collishaw, who received credit that day for six Albatros D Vs claimed OOC. This was not premeditated lying to inflate his claims, just a result of the natural fog of war. As Collishaw recalled about that fight in his 1973 book *Air Command, A Fighter Pilot's Story*:

In a dogfight things happened quickly. You might get in a good shot and see the hostile fighter fall off on one wing and go down, but you would not be able to follow up your attack, for a pair of his fellows would be on your own tail. You might see out of the corner of your eye an enemy machine going down, hopelessly out of control, but you would perhaps have little time to determine which member of your flight had been responsible. Much of this sort of information came to light only after returning to base, listening to the accounts of the other members of your flight.

I got in several bursts at one of the red Albatros fighters from its rear flank and it went down. It seemed that I had hit the pilot, but had no chance at all to follow up for I had to take violent evasive action to avoid being shot up myself. Before the fight was over I sent five more down, each one seemingly out of control. Whether they recovered or not I have no idea, for on not a single occasion did I have a chance to follow up or see whether my victim kept on falling.

In actuality, only von Richthofen's machine had gone down prior to 10 Naval Squadron's arrival – or had it? A luxury of fighting over one's lines was that an emergency landing meant an aeroplane could very well be salvageable and not considered a total loss. Capture was not automatic, and the pilots usually rejoined their *Staffeln* to fight again. Still, did the Germans have at least nine Albatros D Vs shot down or even rendered out of control during the fight of 6 July? Debate over such scoring details continues, and thus credited victories do not necessarily coincide with actual victories. This is true for both sides of World War I, and all other wars. But between the FE 2 and various Albatros scouts, there is no question there was a ferocious give and take. Each type was dangerous, and each spilled the other's blood.

And each side liked their respective machines – at least initially. Regarding the Albatros, *Jasta* 2's Ltn Erwin Bohme wrote:

> Our new aircraft border likewise on marvelous. Compared to the single-seater, which we flew before Verdun [Fokker Eindecker], they are improved. Their rate-of-climb and turning radius are amazing. It is as if they are living, feeling creatures that understand what the pilot wishes. With them one may risk everything and succeed.

Frederick Libby commented on the manoeuvrability and strength of the FE 2, recalling:

FE 2b 4957 of No. 23 Sqn. Note the transparency of the upper wings. This machine featured a 160hp Beardmore, four-bladed propeller and oleo undercarriage. It was damaged in combat on 6 March 1917 and scrapped eight days later.

Jim Laurier

ENGAGING THE ENEMY

Gunsights on the FE 2b/d and Albatros scouts were very simple affairs – little more than post and ring/bead – although Albatros pilots sometimes fitted their machines with captured tubular Aldis sights. But it is without question that gunsights were not as important for shooting down an enemy machine as was attaining the closest range possible before opening fire. Firing within a few aeroplane lengths obviated the need for any telescopic gunsight and maximised the damaging effects of bullet strikes, since bullets lose less energy over shorter distances than those having to travel longer distances to reach a target.

As Manfred von Richthofen wrote in his Air Combat Operations Manual, 'With one sentence one can settle the topic "Air Combat Tactics" – namely, "I go up to 50 metres to the enemy from behind, aim cleanly, then the opponent falls". One does not need to be a flight artist or a marksman but only to have the courage to fly right up to the opponent'. Yet von Richthofen also wrote that 'a long aerial combat with a completely combat-ready, manoeuvrable two-seater is the most difficult. One attacks the two-seater from behind at great speed, in the same direction he is going. The only way to avoid the adroit observer's field of machine gun fire is to stay calm and put the observer out of action with the first shots. If the opponent goes into a turn, I must be careful to not fly above the enemy aeroplane'.

With the FE 2, German pilots faced aggressive offensive gunnery, served up by at least two flexible machine guns with an enormous field-of-fire that obviated the need to cling to an enemy's tail. And although the engine, propeller and tail created a huge rear blind spot, FE 2 gunners could still direct defensive gunfire rearward by standing in their cockpits and firing back up and over the top wing. This countered high aft approaches, as depicted in Jim Laurier's illustration. Enthusiasts today marvel at the courage of FE 2 observers, who fired their weapons while standing without harnesses in manoeuvring aeroplanes, enduring G-loads in relentless and cold relative winds. However, harnesses and continuous sitting were not options for men ordered and expected to go across enemy lines to fight as FE 2 observers. While such activity at least partly required 'youth's scorn of danger', an observer was far less likely to fall overboard than he was to be wounded or shot to death by attacking Albatrosses.

With its wings, horizontal stabilisers and elevator removed, the Albatros D V in which Manfred von Richthofen was wounded rests where he landed on 6 July. It is still armed, and the repaired tailskid and undercarriage suggest the machine has been prepared for towing, although its ultimate fate is unknown.

We are in the midst of Fokkers, Rolands and the German's pet Albatros. All seem to take a poke at us. I am only able to get a shot at one Albatros with my front gun. My pilot seems to have gone wild. We are all over the skies, with lead hitting our FE 2b from every direction. At 500ft we cross our lines and land in the first vacant space. Our upper, emergency petrol tank in the top plane has been hit and petrol has been flowing out of it, two struts are shot and broken, the top wing is drooping. The pilot's altimeter, peter tube [aka, relief tube] and compass have been ruined, and my back Lewis has been hit. Also, there are holes everywhere, except in us and our engine. I am reminded of this remark – if the Hun doesn't get the pilot or engine, the old FE 2b will stagger home.

By the summer of 1917, however, opinions had evolved. In a letter enquiring about new aeroplane types, Manfred von Richthofen wrote, 'The [Albatros] D V is outdated and so ridiculously inferior to the English single-seaters. But for a year now the people at home have not released any better machine than this lousy Albatros, and have stopped with the Albatros D III, with which I have already fought in the autumn of last year'. In reality, von Richthofen had flown the D I and D II in the autumn of 1916, and had not switched to the D III until January 1917.

Similarly, No. 20 Sqn observer Albert Woodbridge recalled, 'our job was offensive patrolling – in other words, we were supposed to go out and light into any enemy aeroplanes we could find. We knew the Albatros scouts could fly rings around us and shoot hell out of us from that blind spot under our tails. We were like butterflies sent out to insult eagles'.

Statistics reveal that these 'insults' were often effective. FE 2 aces have higher Albatros tallies than Albatros aces have FE 2 tallies, and at a glance there are far more FE 2 Albatros 'killers' than vice versa. However, one must remember that FE 2 pilots and observers shared victories (e.g., one Albatros shot down equalled two victories, one each for the FE 2 crew), and while the FE 2s did shoot down their share of Albatros scouts, it does not mean they dominated their German opponents. A major reason for the greater FE 2 Albatros tally is that the aeroplane was Germany's primary fighter, and thus the type that attacked the FE 2s most often – frequently in overwhelming numbers. Conversely, the Albatros faced a larger assortment of enemy aeroplanes in addition to the FE 2, such as the BE 2s, RE 8s, DH 2s, FE 8s, SPAD VIIs, various types of Nieuport, Sopwith 1½ Strutters and Sopwith Pups, so naturally German victory tallies would be more varied.

Note that the FE 2 Albatros D killer tallies contain mostly Albatros D IIIs and D Vs. This is not because the earlier types did not fight FE 2s – von Richthofen shot down five FE 2s while flying an Albatros D I or D II – but because the early Albatros scouts appeared in fewer numbers than the later models. Additionally, the winter of 1916–17 slowed the pace of aerial combat considerably, after which the Albatros D III was present in large numbers. Indeed, by the end of June 1917 there were more than 700 Albatros D IIIs and D Vs at the front, but only 100+ Albatros D Is and D IIs.

Finally, many Albatros scouts were shot down by FE 2 crews who never attained ace status, and just as many FE 2s are attributable to German non-aces. Thus, the statistics supplied here offer but a glimpse of the complete picture, although the dominance of No. 20 Sqn dovetails with its status as the highest-claiming British squadron, just as *Jastas* 2 and 11 dominate German claims.

Leading FE 2 Albatros D I/D V Killers (credited victories)

Pilot	Squadron	D I	D II	D III	D V	Alb Ds	Total Victories
Frederick Thayre	20	-	-	17	--	17	20
Oliver Vickers	20	-	-	2	11	13	13
Richard Trevethan	20	-	-	4	8	12	12
Henry Luchford	20	-	-	9	1	10	24
Cecil Richards	20	-	-	1	9	10	12
Donald Cunnell	20	-	-	3	6	9	9
Harold Satchell	20	-	-	5	3	8	8
Reginald Makepeace	20	-	-	6	2	8	17
James Leith	25	-	4	2	-	6	9
William Durrand	20	-	-	1	3	4	8
Victor Huston	18	-	2	1	1	4	6

Obs/Gunner	Squadron	D 1	D II	D III	D V	Alb D	Total Victories
Francis Cubbon	20	-	-	19	-	19	21
John Cowell	20	-	-	6	8	14	16
Campbell Hoy	20	-	-	-	10	10	10
Archibald Jenks	20	-	-	1	6	7	7
Melville Waddington	20	-	-	-	7	7	12
Albert Wear	20	-	-	1	6	7	9
James Tennant	20	-	-	2	4	6	7
William Cambray	20	-	-	2	3	5	6
Albert Woodbridge	20	-	-	-	4	4	7
Frank Johnson	22	2	1	-	-	3	16

Many FE 2s were employed as night bombers, such as No. 100 Sqn's FE 2b A852 seen here 'bombed up' prior to a night mission. Painted black, its payload includes underwing Cooper bombs and a 230lb bomb under the nacelle. A flare chute protrudes from the nose.

Leading Albatros D I/D V FE 2 Killers (credited victories)

Pilot	Jasta(s)	FE 2b	FE 2d	FE 2s	Total Victories
Manfred von Richthofen	2, 11	11	1	12	80
Walter Göttsch	8	-	7	7	20
Karl Schaefer	11	4	3	7	30
Werner Voss	2	6	1	7	48
Oswald Boelcke	2	4	-	4	40
Edmund Nathanael	5	3	1	4	15
Lothar von Richthofen	11	2	2	4	40
Adolf Ritter von Tutschek	2, 12	1	2	3	27
Hans Klein	4	1	1	2	22

AFTERMATH

FE 2s and Albatros Ds fought until nearly autumn 1917, soldiering on while waiting for superseding designs to be put into production. For the British, one such aeroplane was the Bristol F 2A (aka Bristol Fighter, or 'Biff'). The availability of synchronisation permitted its boxy mid-gap fuselage to be of tractor configuration, with a single forward-firing Vickers 0.303in. machine gun for the pilot and flexible Lewis for the observer. The prototype flew in September 1916 – the month the Albatros Ds arrived in France – although it naturally had to endure a process of tests and redesigns.

In December, 50 production F 2As were delivered to No. 48 Sqn, which trained with the machines until it deployed to France in March 1917. However, on their first patrol on 5 April, six F 2As encountered Albatros D IIIs of *Jasta* 11 led by Manfred von Richthofen. Instead of fighting the Germans offensively, as the type subsequently would throughout the war, the F 2As employed defensive two-seater tactics and four were shot down – some crews also reported problems firing their Lewis guns. Following this one-sided clash, von Richthofen wrote that they had attacked 'a new type of aeroplane that we had not seen as yet – it appears to be quick and rather handy', yet opined, 'the [Albatros] D III, both in speed and in ability to climb, is undoubtedly superior.' Despite this tragic beginning, 200 further F 2As were ordered and ultimately the design begat the F 2B. In all, some 4,700 'Biffs' were built, of which 3,100 saw wartime service.

Bristol F 2A A-3312. Despite the type's disastrous combat debut in April 1917, a change in tactics and development of the improved F 2B ensured the 'Brisfit' was a successful design and worthy of FE 2 succession.

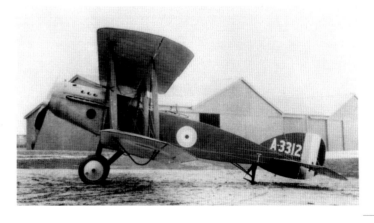

Fokker D VII 244/18. By the time this type arrived in the frontline in the spring of 1918, Albatros pilots were more than ready to welcome it. Free of structural complications that hamstrung Fokker's preceding and succeeding designs, the D VII combined good strength and manoeuvrability.

For the Germans, although the Albatros firm continuously redesigned its D-models to improve performance, each new fighter fell short of expectations. However, life support arrived in the form of the *Amerikaprogramm*, Germany's reaction to the United States' declaration of war against it in April 1917. The Germans believed the weight of US might would not be felt for a year, but began planning immediately, calling in part for an increase of 40 *Jagdstaffeln*. Production output in Germany was already considered to be running at full capacity, and thus great changes were needed to boost monthly aeroplane production by an expected 100 per cent. Furthermore, an emphasis was placed upon the design and production of a new fighter and high-performance aeroplane engine. Until such time, Albatros fighters were already in production and naturally their demand facilitated continued production, despite the Albatros D III's structural problems with the lower wings.

Meanwhile, as the Bristol F 2A began sorties in France, Albatros commenced production of the new D V in its Johannisthal factory near Berlin, while D III production continued via the *Ostdeutsche Albatros Werke* in Schneidmühl (today Pila, in Poland). This doubled the output of fighters, with the added bonus of OAW's construction refinements to rectify the structural weaknesses of their Johannisthal brethren. By the time OAW finished production of its D III, the company had built 60 per cent more D IIIs than Johannisthal.

Afterwards, the two factories began producing the Albatros D Va, the final and most-produced variant of the Albatros D lineage, with some 1,060 D Vas and 600 D Va (OAW)s built. This was another effort to continue and enhance the series, yet the lack of performance increase disappointed pilots who were already dissatisfied with what was considered to be an 'old' machine, although the Albatros D-series had been available only slightly more than a year.

In late summer and early autumn 1917 the Pfalz D III and Fokker Dr I, respectively, arrived, but the latter's immediate grounding due to fatal structural failures meant the Albatros would remain in service. In April 1918, long after the FE 2 had faded from squadron service, more than 1,200 Albatros D III, D V and D Va types were still being used by frontline units. This was their zenith. Although some served until the war's end seven months hence, the arrival of the Fokker D VII finally gave the German pilots the replacement scout they had sought and long anticipated.

FURTHER READING

BOOKS

Bronnenkant, L. J., *The Imperial German Eagles in World War I*, (Schiffer Books, 2006)

Bruce, J. M., *RAF FE 2b*, (Windsock Datafile 18, 1998)

Cross & Cockade Society, *FE 2b/d & Variants in FRC, RAF, RNAS & AFC Service*, (Cross and Cockade International, 2009)

Franks, N., *Jagdstaffel Boelcke* (Grub Street, 2004)

Grosz, P. M., *Albatros D.I/D.II* (Windsock Datafile 100, Albatros Publications, 2003)

Grosz, P. M., *Albatros D.III* (Albatros Publications, 2003)

Guttman, J., *Osprey Aircraft of the Aces 88 – Pusher Aces of World War 1*, (Osprey Publishing, 2009)

Hare, P. R., *RAF FE 2b at War*, (Windsock Datafile 147, Albatros Publications, 2011)

Hare, P. R., *RAF FE 2d*, (Windsock Datafile 134, Albatros Publications, 2009)

Hare, P. R., *The Royal Aircraft Factory*, (Conway Maritime Press, 1990)

Höfling, R., *Albatros D II: Germany's Legendary World War I Fighter* (Schiffer Books, 2002)

Kilduff, P., *The Red Baron* (Doubleday, 1969)

Kilduff, P., *Red Baron: The Life and Death of an Ace* (David & Charles Ltd, 2007)

Lewis, G. H., *Wings Over the Somme 1916–1918* (William Kimber & Co. Ltd, 1976)

Libby, F., *Horses Don't Fly* (Arcade Publishing, Inc., 2000)

McCudden, J., *Flying Fury – Five Years in the Royal Flying Corps* (Greenhill, 2000)

Miller, J. F., *Manfred von Richthofen: The Aircraft, Myths and Accomplishments of 'The Red Baron'* (Air Power Editions, 2009)

Owers, C. A., *Albatros D.V/D.Va at War, Vol 1*, (Windsock Datafile 151, Albatros Publications, 2012)

Owers, C. A., *Albatros D.V/D.Va at War, Vol 2*, (Windsock Datafile 151, Albatros Publications, 2012)

Van Wyngarden, G., *Osprey Aviation Elite Units 26 – Jagdstaffel 2 'Boelcke' – Von Richthofen's Mentor* (Osprey Publishing, 2007)

Van Wyngarden, G., *Osprey Aviation Elite Units 16 – 'Richthofen's Circus' – Jagdgeschwader Nr 1* (Osprey Publishing, 2004)

MAGAZINE ARTICLE

Miller, J. F., 'Eagles vs. Butterflies', *Over the Front*, Vol. 23, No. 3, Autumn 2008, pp. 196–214

INDEX

References to illustrations are shown in **bold**. References to plates are shown in **bold** with caption pages in brackets, e.g. **60–61** (62–63).